P9-DCS-196

Contents

Foreword

While the characteristics of Asperger syndrome could imply that a successful relationship is elusive, *Asperger Syndrome – A Love Story* will give encouragement to those who have yet to experience such a relationship, and help them to recognise that they are lovable. Men with Asperger syndrome can be very attractive to a certain type of woman and Sarah is one of those women. She naturally understands the way a person with Asperger syndrome thinks and she speaks the language of Asperger syndrome as a second language. Keith, her partner with Asperger syndrome, is attracted to Sarah for many reasons, but in particular she helps him understand the social aspects of life, and he is able to be himself when he is with her.

Asperger Syndrome – A Love Story was written to provide both insight into the thinking of each partner in an unconventional relationship, and constructive strategies to lead to a more satisfying relationship for both parties. As I read the thoughts and comments of Sarah and Keith, I learned valuable information on how having Asperger syndrome affects a relationship, and appreciated the modifications that are needed to make the relationship work and benefit both partners. The reader very quickly appreciates the difficulties faced by Sarah and Keith and their biography of their relationship is engaging, informative and encouraging. I know that couples (especially those in the early stages of a relationship between a man or woman with Asperger syndrome and a neurotypical partner) will appreciate the story. They will identify with Sarah and Keith, and with their thoughts and experiences, and will find it helpful to adopt many of the strategies.

Tony Attwood
March 2007

Preface

Sarah

Picture the scene, if you will. I am on the bus to work, listening to Barry Manilow on my MP3 player (it's a weakness, I confess). I am struck by a plan and a burst of romance. I send my love a text: 'When I am 40, I would like to go to Las Vegas, marry you and go and see Barry'. I am not expecting much – perhaps 'Oh, darling, how romantic and forward-thinking you are' – but not this: 'How about you marry Johnny Vegas in Barry (Glamorgan)?'

I am in love with a man with Asperger syndrome. Welcome to my world.

There seem to be plenty of women out there who have fallen for a man like this. I have read all of the books, many hundreds of online forum postings and attended seminars. The overwhelming message seems to be one of doom. These women are in despair: resentful, unsupported, angry and depressed. Some women on these forums had left their partner some years ago, but yet they seem unable to move forward and away. Some have even developed characteristics defined as a separate syndrome, Cassandra Affective Disorder, purely as a result of their time with these partners (Aston 2005). The prognosis seems to be universal: being in a relationship with a partner with Asperger syndrome (AS) is likely to result in depression, anxiety and low self-esteem. Your family and friends won't believe that your quiet, gentle, hard-working man is a cold, distant, selfish pedant. He may tell you that it must be you; that you are quite mad, over-sensitive, that you pick fights and cause trouble. I know those feelings only too well, recognise the presence of Cassandra in my own life, have doubted my sanity to the point of despair and heard myself defend my right to be upset a thousand times. Despite all this, I do believe that a relationship like this can work because we now are happily doing so, not without considerable effort, upheaval and compromise, but we're very happy and it's great.

I am lucky enough to work in the field of Asperger syndrome so have the opportunity to meet quite a few individuals with these traits and to learn a great deal. I must add that Keith pre-dates my work in this area – I didn't find him at work and take him home with me. People often say to me in the AS training sessions I deliver as part of my job: 'All men are like that' when they hear the characteristics of the condition. It's true that many men seem to exhibit these AS traits, but this does not adequately reflect the level of impairment that many people with AS have in their difficulty or inability to reach many of the expected milestones of life – job, relationship, self-care, friends. This idea of it being a male-brained condition is explained by Simon Baron-Cohen's work on the extreme male brain theory of autism (Baron-Cohen 2003). He suggests that those on the autistic spectrum demonstrate typical male behaviours but to a more concentrated degree. This is not like most men, or women for that matter. Many may have a few ticks in a few AS trait boxes without it impacting on their ability to participate in life in a significant way.

As it is such an invisible disability, expectations of Keith are high because he is clever, has a job and doesn't look different to the casual observer, so surely he can cope with having a conversation, taking on board someone else's opinion or certain foods on his plate? It is difficult for people to understand how overwhelming he finds certain occasions or situations without it sounding as though I am making excuses for him to do as he pleases or making him seem like a selfish, uncaring bastard.

I learned a huge amount about Keith in the compiling of this book and this knowledge has helped to further strengthen our relationship. There have been other occasions when I have been reminded that some things have not changed in our time together and probably never will. I am slightly concerned that I shall come out of this looking less than good, but so be it. I have not requested any edits from Keith in order to make myself look better and neither has he. If that's what he thought, then it should be included, and on the whole I have found his insights enlightening and funny. His way of expressing himself is so 'him', and I can see him saying or writing these things in my mind. We have chosen not to avoid some of the painful areas as this felt dishonest and unhelpful. In order to share and learn, we felt the need to present as full a picture as possible. We also wanted to try and bring a sense of ourselves rather than be too stuffy. I hope that this book makes for a good read rather than just an informative piece.

The level of self-awareness that Keith has shown has astounded me. From total denial to acceptance has taken around two years and has been a tough ride. I am in awe of his willingness to write this book with me. He is intensely private, and I thought that he wouldn't want to commit his life for all to see, but then I am often wrong about him and often underestimate him. I should know better.

Keith

I don't know exactly why I've contributed to this book. Well, for two simple reasons I do:

First, Sarah (my partner and the focus of my attention in this book) has recently become interested in the subject of Asperger syndrome due to our mutual discovery that I undoubtedly (in my opinion) am affected by this condition, and has found a career for herself in the field. One of the many things that attracted me to her is her amazing ability to see what others can't. It was her brainchild that we write this book. Even though I didn't get the purpose, I could see no substantive reason not to contribute and help fulfil her ambition of being successfully published in this field. I would never have imagined that something so central (normal) to me could ever be the core subject for a book, and I still struggle to see why this would be of interest to anyone.

Second, I get a percentage share of the profits of the book sales. I couldn't possibly turn down the opportunity of earning a bit of cash for the simple task of writing about something I know a lot about, i.e. me.

It has become apparent through the course of writing for this book that there might be an element of public service that we are providing here (actually, this is what Sarah knew all along!). It is mostly for the people without AS in relationships with people with AS – those in Sarah's situation. One of the main purposes of this book is to provide some insight into the thinking of people with AS. Of course, if the non-AS partner can get an appreciation for the AS, then this might lead to an overall more satisfying relationship for both parties. I hope it works out like that.

I can't recall what I have learned about myself through contributing to this work. I have, though, learned more about my co-author. It transpires she knows and understands the thought process of AS (and therefore me) a lot, lot better than I imagined. This makes the world a lot better place to be in.

Introduction – Setting the Scene

The structure of the book follows our increasing understanding. It begins with explanations of who we are as individuals, chronicles our meeting and first ill-fated relationship, followed by a painful but vital period of separation and learning to the final destination of a new, different, more satisfactory relationship together. This doesn't always fit neatly into chapter headings, despite our best attempts; there are overlaps, repetitions and bits that seem to fit nowhere – much like AS itself.

From our reading and experience, we believe that a considerable amount of what we have experienced is common to other couples in our position, and we hope that this will be useful for others to know that they are not alone with these thoughts and feelings and that, perhaps, there is a way to minimise the stress of this type of relationship – for both parties. There is no intention to claim that we smugly know what's right or that we have got it sussed; far from it. From having started out together with a difficult, confusing relationship that fell apart very painfully, we have managed to build a different one. We have seen both sides.

This book is not a piece of objective research; it is a personal account. We seek to attempt to redress the high level of bad press for AS relationships and present the positive side. We are, without doubt, happier together than apart. All relationships are difficult – we know of no 'normal' couples who experience any fewer problems than we do; all couples misread and misunderstand each other. When we look around at our friends and peers, we see people struggling with their relationships.

This book is written from the perspective of an AS male with a non-AS female partner. We acknowledge the huge lack of resources for other AS partnership combinations but do not have the experience to address these here. We use 'AS' as a shortened form of 'Asperger syndrome' and 'non-AS' for the other partner. We do not wish to get involved in arguments of terminology.

This book assumes a basic knowledge of the characteristics of AS and their impact on individuals, although this is covered to some extent. Sarah has a degree of professional knowledge in this area and has added this where appropriate to demonstrate typically seen traits in a more generalised way rather than always just referring to Keith. No two people with AS will display the diagnostic characteristics in the same way or to the same degree, due to differences in the condition and also in personality, background and many other factors. We concur with this here: Keith is a one-off and whilst some of his behaviour and thoughts may ring bells with readers, others may not. That's the way this thing works.

During the time that we have known each other, Keith has changed enormously and in many ways is not as 'Asperged' as he used to be. He does seem to be comfortable in many situations now. This was not always the case. We had a very difficult Relationship Mk I and now have a very different Relationship Mk II. One of us is 'better' now because the other is 'better' now. Demands are not being placed upon Keith and so he is able to be more available than he would otherwise. We mention this in case readers feel that he is less affected than their own partners, which has not necessarily always been the case. He certainly will be affected differently to anyone else's partner. We believe that changes in both partners are possible to mutual good.

It is also worth mentioning that we do not currently live together and never have. Living together is often seen as a mark of progress or commitment and we would like to challenge that notion. We can be equally committed in separate houses. We spend three days each week together on average, where we are usually together 24/7, although do have periods apart when other commitments get in the way. We acknowledge that many people who are living with their partner have additional issues that we do not have. Perhaps it is necessary to re-define expectations of living arrangements or of the relationship itself due to the large amounts of solitude or down-time that some individuals with AS require. The

ability to be separate may be a key factor in the success of this relationship, and we make no excuse for that.

It was originally thought that this book would be on the whole a
joint effort with each of us contributing entire chapters independently.
This has turned out not to be the case and has been a useful learning
experience in itself. Keith has found it impossible to know what to write
when left to his own devices because he doesn't know that many of the
things about him are unusual or of interest. He lacks the ability to see
another perspective – which is part of the condition. He has found it
time-consuming and exhausting to examine his own thoughts and put
them into coherent words and has required a lot of support to do so.
Hence, the topics covered in this book have been mostly guided by Sarah,
who has written her thoughts on situations which she believes to be
indicative of AS and where she feels that his insight may prove valuable or
interesting to others. He has then generally responded to those
comments. The end result has meant far more of this book has been
written by Sarah, which was not the original intention. Everything that
we have written has been mutually edited and agreed.

There is no intention to offend or deride anyone with AS. We find
some aspects of how AS affects Keith funny; that's not to say that this is
generalised over the entire autistic community – it's just us. It means we
are comfortable with our own peculiarities and embrace them – a
personal choice. We would say or do nothing which did not demonstrate
the utmost respect for each other. If our sense of humour is off the mark
for some readers, we apologise.

CHAPTER 1

How Did I Get Here?

K: Most people I've known for a long time will testify that
    I'm a bit strange in a universally indescribable way...just
    weird.

Sarah's mum: You're like a bull in a china shop.

Keith

Maybe when young we only have the ability to retain memories that are
significant to us on an emotional basis. When older we are able to apply
other emotions to the process of storing memories and remember other
less significant stuff. My early memories mostly fall into two categories:
good and bad. (Actually this is a fair insight into life in general: if
thinking is polar; it's easier to cope.)

There are few things I remember from my childhood. There are
photo albums, but I don't know if what is triggered in my head when I see
them are real or invented memories, by which to place myself in the pho-
tographs. I remember the boy next door and recall his name; there are
black and white pictures of me in my broken spectacles with my arm
around his shoulders. He moved house one day and was replaced by
another boy. I never really liked him much: he wasn't the other boy, but
he was there and I had to get on with him. He was strange, he had old
parents and his mother died one day. He was a year older than me. There
were seven other children of similar age around, so lots of people who I
could be friends with. I'm sure I was sociable. Days were nearly always
spent kicking balls, exploring the woods, digging in soil, and sometimes
eating it, roaming the hills and in each other's houses.

I remember being clumsy, which remains today. My parents were incredulous and took it quite personally that I would break plates and cups, as well as stubbing my toes. Surprisingly, there were no broken bones! Today I've moderated my behaviour so that almost every movement is controlled, every footfall is placed carefully; it's all so contrived, but is the only way to prevent damage and injury. It feels confining and imprisoning, yet is the only tactic that works; as soon as I let go, or concentrate on anything other than the movement in hand, I get hurt or things get broken. It is an exhausting way to live, but necessary.

Primary school was a small, 200-pupil place, where just about everyone knew each other. Some of the people in this school were the children with whom I played. There were others too. Everyone was happy. It was an idyll. Comprehensive school was a 1200-pupil affair. Most of the people who had been in my primary school were dispersed within other classes. I didn't understand why. In my class of 30 I was the kid who stood out for all the wrong reasons: I was tall, thin, with red hair, glasses, bright, uncoordinated and uncomfortable in my own skin. The first attention this brought was the physical pecking order: the thugs in my class were mostly preoccupied with who could hit others the hardest, so being the tallest in the class I attracted a whole heap of unwanted attention. I'd hoped that my complete lack of interest in walloping anyone would have put paid to that, but it only seemed to confuse them. The number of unprovoked thumpings I received I cannot count. The most bizarre was Tae Kwon Do Paul, who insisted that I hit him, or he would hit me…surely if I hit him though he would retaliate, and I had no interest in being hit at all? He hit me. The second most bizarre was being dragged along to find Johnny M (who was a bit of an egghead) and being forced (under threat of violence) to ask each other hard questions to see who was the brightest. I have read that bullying is a very common occurrence in children (and adults) with AS.

These events just happened to me. It didn't feel natural that they should, but they did, and that didn't give me the right to question it: if someone does something then it must be for a reason. (I recall a conversation in later life which revealed quite a disparity between my approach to life and that of others. I found that most people reply with 'Why not?' when given the chance to do something, anything, whereas my approach is a definite 'Why do anything?') I always felt that I didn't have a right to intervene; that others had the right to do entirely what they wanted to me. (**Sarah**: The advent of secondary education coinciding with puberty is often the time when AS becomes apparent and begins to cause problems as the individual is thrust into a bigger social world of less forgiving souls – up to 90 per cent of children with AS are reported to suffer bullying of some description (Attwood 2006).)

Throughout the years there I got to know a number of good people. I didn't socialise with any of them. I didn't socialise at all and had no desire to. I have no recollection of what I used to spend my time doing. Once or twice I was asked out or invited to local discos by females, but they were all kidding and involved in some extended form of insult like almost everyone else, right? Right? I was aware that others were mixing socially. I just thought: 'That is what other people do, not me.' It was just a simple fact; a truth, like 'Why is the sky blue?' It just is. Summer holidays were mostly spent cycling around the country on a tandem with my father, or spent by myself.

After studying for A-levels at school I went to university and lived in halls of residence for the entire three years because I couldn't tolerate the process of looking after myself, for instance cooking. This was done for me in halls – we ate communally in the dining room. I had no contact with any fellow students outside of eating together for those three years. I was not bullied or bothered, merely left alone. I knew that other people were going out socially together, and I would have liked to join them but had no idea how to make this happen, and my perceived difficulty in trying to make it happen was insurmountable. I still felt resigned to the fact that this happened to others and not me. I was attracted to women but never did anything about it. How could I? Why would anyone want to go out with me? I couldn't see that they would, so I didn't bother.

After university, I spent six months in Australia with someone who had gone to some of the same lectures as me. I don't regard us as having a friendship, as such. I wasn't fazed by doing this trip as I had organised long cycling trips staying at youth hostels in the UK and this didn't seem to be any different. On my return, I stayed with my parents until I began work in my current field of sonar. I had to move to the south coast from the north of England to do so. Once I had done so, I pretty much shut myself off from the world for about seven years. It wasn't deliberate, it just happened, like much in my life. I went to work and came home. I read no newspapers, watched no television and listened to no music, only Radio 4. I still cannot recognise songs that were released during this period. I went to a small independent cinema and watched films. Throughout this period I remember having thoughts of trying to train my mind not to become emotionally attached to anyone, and to live a self-fulfilled (isolated) existence. I wished I was sexless and led a monastic life. I had one friend from work who would invite me to go visit him occasionally. I never invited him to visit me because I didn't know that is what you were supposed to do. When he announced he was to leave the company and the area, I turned to isolation even more strongly. I was distraught and alone again – it was quite a wrench, I'd obviously not taught myself so well.

I began my first relationship at the age of 31 with a woman from work. I imagine that she had shown her interest in me for some time, but I had not really noticed. This relationship lasted for around 18 months. She became very emotional and frustrated that I could not express how I felt about her and had great difficulty communicating with her. This resulted in heated discussions and rows. She felt I was too much of a nightmare to live with; even at the time I could see that she was probably right, but had no idea what I was supposed to be doing to improve the situation. I didn't understand any of this until recently, since I have learned about AS.

I had another couple of brief relationships lasting a couple of months after this, one was someone who lived next door, the other via internet dating, but I either felt that they were too much effort or I couldn't cope when the person expressed their love for me, so I ended them. I was (and to a degree still am) conflicted about relationships. I need my solitude, but know that sharing experiences and having someone to love is enjoyable.

In November 2003, I saw Sarah on an internet dating site. Encountering Sarah has proved to be life-changing. It was apparent from the very first communications with her that she was unlike anyone I had met. She was challenging, and I mean that in the very best possible way. She is not passive and accepting of what life throws at her. It is by her probing that I am here today, more self-aware than I have ever been and with a satisfactory explanation for my individualism. Maybe I would have gotten to this point alone, but maybe not. There might not have been enough time in my life to do it without her.

Sarah

I include myself for background and to show the obvious part of my own character and baggage that I bring to cloud the water in this partnership. Both Tony Attwood (2006) and Maxine Aston (2003) ascertain that certain types of women are attracted to the AS man, and I have no doubt that I fall firmly into one of these categories. These women tend to be super-empathisers, nurturers, strong and capable. With hindsight, I am staggered to see how many people with AS traits have been in my life. And all that time I thought I was making free choices! Recently, I discovered that Gary Numan has AS. I had a huge crush on him, aged 11. How could I possibly have known! Something about him – the aloofness, his soft attractiveness, the lack of overt sexuality and machismo obviously triggered something even back then.

A key moment of clarity regarding my own experience came around six months after meeting Keith. I knew he was unusual, and AS had been mentioned by a friend of mine, but the full implications were as yet unclear to either of us. I remember sitting in his flat musing on why I felt so at ease around him and who he was like from my past. I pondered on the popular psychological notion that people tend to be attracted to partners who are similar to one of their parents (usually a father for a woman). This is said to be due to the fact that there is a familiarity which we are drawn to and also that any unresolved issues with that parent (lack of affection, abuse, etc.) will be relived through the new partner, because (bizarrely) feeling bad in that way is comfortingly reassuring too. I considered the comparison between Keith and my dad. There was little. I was puzzled. My father was a noisy, physically strong, Liverpudlian, could talk to anyone, always laughing and seeing the best in life. Here in front of me was a pale, abnormally skinny, effeminate man who had led the most extremely isolated and non-social existence I had ever encountered. It didn't fit. Where was the pattern? Where was the hook? Why was I here? And then the penny dropped; this wasn't about my dad at all – it was my mum. It had never occurred to me that I may have chosen partners because of my mother, but from that moment onwards lots of things have all fallen into place for me.

I have subsequently examined this more closely along with the developing understanding of Keith's AS and now believe very strongly that my mum had significant elements of AS. She died in 2001 so my thoughts are largely unproven. Mum was quite an eccentric character; but this was tolerated and respected in her generation. Having any kind of diagnosis would not have benefited her in any way. She had all the milestones of a successful and full life for a woman of her generation – marriage, kids, part-time job and a well-kept home. It has been said that those with AS who grew up pre-1950s have fared much better than those of a younger generation due to having fewer expectations and choices. AS was not recognised in the UK until the late 1970s. Life was more straightforward; choice of job was more limited. Perhaps people were more tolerant of others without requiring labels.

My mother was seen to be very shy, she had few friends throughout her life – her closest, and only real friend, a woman she had known for her entire 70 odd year life, she was never on first name terms with, still referring to her as 'Mrs'. She only wore black, white or grey clothes. I always imagined this to be out of habit, but after seeing a programme on TV about Temple Grandin, the autistic woman who designs amazing slaughterhouses for cows using her exceptional visualisation skills (Grandin 1995) and who also wears the same clothes every day, I understand that it means not having to worry about what to wear. Not having to think about whether things match or go together.

She had a very restricted diet throughout her adult life, consisting almost exclusively of cheese sandwiches and tea. She found no enjoyment in food and only ate because she had to. I have met others with AS who eat quite unvaried foods. Reducing the need for thought or anxiety in certain areas makes life easier for people with AS, which is why many have rituals and routines for things they do daily: 'I know I like cheese sandwiches, so it is predictable. If I think about having something else, I may not like it or may not have the required ingredients, so best to stick with what is known.'

She had a phenomenal memory and could recount physical details of her childhood home to an amazing degree. She could recall how many stairs there were between each floor, the location of the light switches and the colour and pattern of wallpaper in every room. Her descriptions were very vivid and suggest a strong visual memory often ascribed to people with AS and mentioned by Temple Grandin (1995) as one of her strongest features.

Despite continually telling me how clumsy I was, she herself was known to be highly destructive. She went through kettles and irons like there was no tomorrow, always managing to break them. She would not ask for help in doing heavy tasks, even into her 70s. If she wanted something doing, she would not wait until help was available, she would do it herself, even when it was clearly not safe to do so. Mum once carried a sheet of wood, 8' x 4' in size, balanced on the top of her shopping trolley the mile or so home from the DIY store. My father had worked with power tools in his job and she had kept this huge, industrial electric saw after he had died. She decided one day that she needed to cut a piece of wood, didn't bother to get the work bench out of the shed or ask my brother who lived nearby, so just laid the piece of wood on the floor to cut it, resting her foot on it to keep it still. Needless to say she wasn't strong enough to brace against the kick of this enormously powerful saw and it bounced off into her foot. She was about 72 at the time. She was fine about it, still didn't accept that doing things differently might have been a good idea and couldn't see the fuss everyone was making about how dangerous it had been.

She had a strong sensitivity to smell – certain things made her gag and retch. At the time it seemed that she was over-reacting to something fairly minor. Her reaction was quite inappropriate; she would loudly screech her disgust wherever she was and almost vomit. This reaction was not caused by anything really revolting – being given a cup of coffee instead of tea, or eating a doughnut with too much sugar on would do it. She hated the countryside because it was smelly. Whenever we drove past a field of cows she would hastily reach in her bag for her Olbas Oil (a strong-smelling mixture of plant oils including eucalyptus and clove), shake a few drops on to a tissue (of which she always had many stuffed up each sleeve 'just in case') and cover her nose and mouth with it and inhale. It was like her reaching for her mask in times of gas attack – a desperate flurry of activity in order to eliminate the poison (cow poo). It was considered weird and funny by my family, but no more than that. She was never really able to express how awful it must have been to her in a way we could appreciate.

Mum found being with lots of people very difficult. She would sit in the kitchen alone when people came round, she would never attend my father's work parties – my sister went instead. At my own wedding, you can see her straight, unsmiling face in amongst the other guests (she hated having her photo taken). Watching Temple Grandin on TV in a similar role brought this back to me very strongly as I had forgotten about this physical characteristic. She never popped in unannounced into neighbours' houses, like they all did to each other, she was very private and self-contained.

As a parent, she was utterly dedicated to providing care for us. I am the youngest by 15 years so spent much of my childhood as virtually an only child as my siblings were at college by then. Mum had never wanted to have any children and quite openly said so. She also said that she would prefer not to be here (i.e. alive) and if she could find a guaranteed way to resolve that then she would take it. I often felt very sad for her and assumed that she must have been terribly depressed and was crying for help. There never seemed to be any emotion when she said these types of things, and with the knowledge I have now I believe that these were simply facts or truths for her. I have met other people with AS who express similar thoughts in a similarly factual way. When I would be upset by her saying these things, she would look genuinely bewildered that there was any emotional impact on a 13-year-old child, tell me not to be so silly and wonder what was I getting upset about. This is very much my experience of some people with AS – they simply tell the truth and have no concept of whether it is appropriate or helpful to do so. The truth is all and no one can possibly have any issue with it, as it is an inescapable thing. I have no issue with my mum. She did the best she could with what she had. She would never have intentionally harmed me and would have been distraught if she had known that it had any detrimental effect. She was a stubborn, cantankerous moo who infuriated her family with her inflexibility – she would not budge once she had decided on something, regardless of the evidence against it – but she was, and is, greatly loved and missed, and the source material for many strange and funny stories due to her peculiar ways! There are many more examples of her AS-like behaviours but this is not the place for them.

My life has been so different to Keith's that it makes me wonder how we have anything in common. I suppose I am a psychoanalyst's dream, finding peace and happiness with a man who exhibits the same character-istics as my mother! I include the detail purely for contrast to Keith's life as mine has been substantially different. What follows is a brief summary of an eventful life.

I was feted as a 'gifted' child, and everyone around me had high expectations of my potential, especially in language and literature. I apparently spoke full sentences by nine months of age, wrote short stories, entered poetry competitions and performed well at school with little effort. I was very shy as a child. From growing up on a Surrey council estate, I won a scholarship to a private school and was set to go on to great things. Somewhere in my mid-teens, however, I realised that I had no desire to do what was planned for me. I scraped through my O-levels on intelligence rather than any effort, left school at 16 and went to live in a squat in London with a boyfriend. By 19, I was a single parent to my daughter. I got married at 21 to an older man and moved to Lancashire. The marriage lasted a year. I went to college and did a couple of A-levels and ended up at university in Devon. I hated my course, lasted two years and dropped out. I met someone else and eventually we had a son and got married. That relationship ended after 12 years. During this time I had a random series of part-time jobs, including writing a cookery book (Sanderson 1994), as I felt that my place was with my children and that their needs came before my own – an immovable belief that I have inherited from my mother. Since the end of my second marriage several years ago, and the increasing ages of my children – my daughter has now left home, my son is almost a teenager and lives partly with his dad – I have finally started to spend some time by myself deciding what I would like to do and establishing a 'career' of sorts for myself. Perhaps unsurprisingly, this has led me to work in the area of disability teaching, and ultimately AS. I worked for several years in a college supporting and teaching learners with disabilities, some of whom had AS, and yet I never spotted this in those in my personal life.

Purely by chance I saw an advertisement in my local paper for my current job as Training Manager for a new project working with AS adults. I applied and was successful. The project offers support and mentoring, and I also deliver awareness training to organisations in what AS is and how best to support people with it. I wouldn't have my current job had I not met Keith and learned so much about him and the condition. When I saw it advertised I knew this job was made for me. I love what I do and work in a fantastic environment. It has also given me access to a large amount of training, which has had a hugely important and positive impact on my life with Keith and my understanding of other people in my life. It's been an unusual but valuable journey in many ways.

Sometimes, I feel like I speak Asperger as a second language. My upbringing from my mother was one of having my practical care needs being met but not so my emotional needs. I certainly have not inherited AS from her; I have a good imagination and a high degree of intuition and perception with regard to other people. I am adaptable and flexible and can deal with uncertain situations and love the notion of change and new experiences. I can easily read body language and facial expressions. I believe that I have learned a lot of my no-nonsense approach to life from my mother, who had no patience for time wasting or dawdling. I am sometimes said to be intolerant and have little time for those who say they will do something and then don't. I seem to lack the necessity to adhere to some social boundaries and am bewildered by the reactions of others who find this outrageous or unusual. I do tend to make inappropriate jokes or comments and am said to be blunt. Where Keith will say 'Why?' I will say 'Why not?' and challenge this notion of inaction, as I see it. Despite this I am very sensitive to the feelings of others and I do worry about having said or done the wrong thing. Many aspects of life make me feel quite anxious, but I generally hide this well. Despite delivering training to groups of strangers and being able to respond to unknown questions very quickly and well, I can struggle badly socially and am sometimes unable to cover this up; I will sit in a corner or just sneak away quietly. Keith and I are not as different as people often imagine.

I know that I am good at translating the world into language and ideas that Keith can understand. I try to explain how other people behave and see things. He is often amazed at what he hears as this has been a mystery to him until now. Sometimes my desire to understand him can allow me to set aside the emotional impact of what he says long enough to realise that it is all OK and that I don't need to feel upset. A childhood with my mum has prepared me well for a thick skin and rational outlook! I very much enjoy the challenge of communicating effectively with Keith. I can feel my brain stretching to its limits to creatively find a way to work out what is going on in his head. Sounds like hard work, I suppose, but I absolutely love it.

CHAPTER 2

Diagnosis

It was the definitive that finally made sense of my life,
the missing piece of me that, once found, made me whole.

Lianne Holliday Willey, on diagnosis (2006, p.20)

Asperger syndrome is a pick-and-mix of traits with each person display-ing different selections to varying degrees. Some traits are barely present, others hugely visible. These all overlap to create an individual whose needs are unique. Because of this variety, there may be many things men-tioned in the following discussion of where Keith ticks the boxes for diagnosis that bear little resemblance to your own experience of someone with AS.

Sarah: Keith would appear on the face of it to be 'normal' as he has achieved many major milestones of life – education, house, career, rela-tionship – but he struggles to do many things that I take for granted. He has also led a very isolated and lonely existence due to his inability to understand and navigate social behaviour.

There is no doubt in my mind or his that Keith has AS. I believe that were he to seek diagnosis he would come out with a full complement of AS traits. He has completed Simon Baron-Cohen's (2003) Autistic Quotient (AQ), Empathy Quotient (EQ) and Systemizing Quotient (SQ) and sits very squarely in the AS bracket. The AQ scores are from 0–60 with a higher score indicating more autistic tendencies. Keith scored 37.

The EQ asks respondents to comment on statements regarding empathy. Again a higher score indicates higher empathy skills. A person with AS would not be expected to perform particularly well in this test. A maximum score of 80 is possible. Keith scored 18. The SQ relates to the systemising qualities, typically said to be good in those with AS. Again the maximum score is 80 and Keith scored 49. I am not an expert in this area and appreciate the subjectivity of this, but it adds to the weight of evidence and justification for writing this book. I was quite shocked at the scores he achieved in these tests as he can appear quite unaffected. To learn how different his answers must have been from my own and the population in general was shocking. Despite the time I have known him and others like him I still find it hard to grasp the difference between how he appears and what is going on in his head.

Any kinds of diagnosis of developmental conditions are fraught with difficulties in adults. Tales of misdiagnosis are common, and Keith has said he sees no benefit in acquiring an 'official' notice from someone who doesn't know him when he happily sees that AS explains his entire life. I have been aware of AS individuals who have been diagnosed as schizo-phrenic (complete with many years of anti-psychotic medication), bipolar depression, attention deficit hyperactivity disorder (ADHD) and obsessive compulsive disorder (OCD). Although there may well be elements of other conditions overlapping for any individual (known as comorbidity), the implications of misdiagnosis may be damaging. Adults with AS have received the signals that they have 'got it wrong' so many times by the time they reach adulthood that they have learned all sorts of strategies and coping mechanisms to hide themselves. Trying to diagnose what is innate and what is learned must be a difficult business. Diagnosis in adults is hard to come by on the NHS in the UK, requiring a referral from an understanding GP, and costly to get privately – around £800. Some people feel that they need to have a diagnosis to be able to use this as evidence to those around them that this is a real condition and needs to be taken seriously. A diagnosis is required if one is to seek access to certain services or welfare benefits on the basis of having AS. Several people that I have worked with are signed on to disability benefits as unable to work on the basis of the depression and anxiety that often comes as a result of living with AS rather than being a characteristic of AS itself. There are so few adult AS support services that I feel an official diagnosis has limited benefits at the moment, especially combined with the difficulties of the adult diagnostic process mentioned above. Self-diagnosis or self-disclosure is increasingly acceptable within the social model of disability. This model does not see the person with a disability in need of a 'cure' or being required to fit society as it is. The model states that the environment makes the person disabled by the lack of access, adequate provision, etc. It is a more accepting ethos where reasonable adjustments are made to allow difference to be appreciated and seen as a positive.

There are several diagnostic tools that set out criteria for diagnosing Asperger syndrome. These include those set out in the Diagnostic and Statistical Manual of Mental Disorders (American Psychiatric Association 1994), those developed by Gillberg (Gillberg 1991), the Australian Scale for Asperger Syndrome (Garnett and Attwood 1991), and the World Health Organisation's International Classification of Diseases (ICD-10) (WHO 2005). The characteristics that we describe below are typical of people with AS, and we have both written our perceptions as Keith is not always aware of how he is seen by other people (this comes across as horribly negative, but then diagnosing a disability or condition by its very nature focuses on impairments or deviations from the norm). I hope it is useful as a measure by which to appreciate what Keith finds tricky – it is not intended to be critical of him.

Difficulty expressing and interpreting non-verbal communication – eye contact, body language and facial expressions – in order to fully understand social communication

Keith: Looking people in the eyes hurts: I don't know what people are thinking or why. The general subject of non-verbal communication is a minefield. After reading a book on body-language recently, I realised that I am atypical – mostly guarded is the message I think I portray. I just wish for some simplicity in communication. This is why telephone is sometimes the perfect way of communicating, because everything that needs to be said, is said – although I am aware that I don't always get the full story without some form of visual feedback that isn't available by telephone.

Sarah: Keith makes less eye contact than most people and sometimes it appears not quite as it should – too long or short, which suggests it is learned behaviour rather than intuitive. He also doesn't seem to be able to read the full extent of facial expressions. It is said that people with AS do not 'read' any information from the eyes, as others do, so see no point in looking at someone in this way, although I have met other people with AS who say that there is too much information and detail in a face and they need to close their eyes or look away in order to focus on their own thoughts.

Keith smiles a lot and laughs, although this sometimes seems like a nervous reaction, as though by smiling it will stop anyone hitting him – possibly a result of years of negative feedback and bullying. He will also laugh randomly and at inappropriate times. I have met other people with AS who barely make any facial expressions and are more intense in their nature, which would make for a different experience. His body language appears defensive at times and guarded, as he says. 'Just awkward' sums it up.

He also has a habit of 'celebrity spotting'. He loudly 'whispers' and points at people who he claims look like someone famous. He was once sworn at by a man who he said (a little too loudly) looked like George Best. He thinks half the population looks like Phil Collins! These people never look anything like the person he says. I wonder if this is perhaps partly due to an inability to distinguish faces – along with poor social skills (both AS characteristics)!

Lack of, and difficulty forming friendships and peer relationships

Keith: Frankly, I have no friends. I know some people. But there is no one I can honestly say I have a relationship with that could be described as a 'friend'. Sometimes I feel it might be useful to have friends, but there again what for? I've never much had these sort of relationships in the past and yet I seem to have managed – anyway, don't they just disappoint and let you down? Mostly, it's simply easier not to bother. It's mostly about not knowing how to do it and the pain of trying and failing far outweighs any benefit that I could possibly perceive coming from friendship.

Sarah: Apart from Keith's immediate family, I have never met anyone that he knows. There are a few people that he sees very intermittently – old work colleagues, I think, but this is less than once a year. I have never been invited to meet any of these people. I find this upsetting, but understand that he just doesn't seem to get it that taking me along is just what people do. He comes across as childlike and self-interested and seems not to understand how friendships work. He views much social conversation or small talk as shallow and pointless as he feels he hasn't learned anything. Some people with AS do have a social network, but often it consists of people who share similar interests and this is the focus of the relationship rather than on a social basis.

As he has said, he shut himself off from the world from 1994 to 2001, apart from going to work. He dropped this into the conversation as though it were the most natural thing in the world. Even in my work, I am not aware of anyone who has isolated themselves quite so much. Keith struggles to realise how unusually isolated his life has been because he has no one to compare it with. He is certainly more willing to socialise with me these days, although I suspect this now causes me more anxiety that it does him as he still seems so awkward and uncomfortable.

Lack of desire or understanding as to the importance of sharing information and activities with others

Keith: I know it must be done – and sometimes I can remember it must, but mostly not. This stems from not caring, not in a deliberately unpleasant way, simply that I am unable to feel any different. This is discussed later in more depth.

Sarah: Keith rarely shares information with others. For example, he wouldn't tell his mum on the phone that he had been away for the weekend with me despite speaking to her at least once a week. Keith rarely suggests activities or plans for us to do, most of the ideas and motivation comes from me. He did book a surprise weekend for us once during the first three months we were together, this has never been repeated. I have no idea how he managed to do it once and then gave up (despite my obvious joy at having been treated in such a special way).

Issues with understanding the two-way nature of relationships and the social world

Keith: This is so difficult. I don't know what to do, when, where or why. Sometimes I wish people wouldn't try to engage me and would just leave me alone. It would make my life so much simpler. Often my initial perception at social gatherings is that I want to flee and escape. Generally, if I hang around for long enough and allow myself to become accustomed to the situation, it is not as horrid as I had preconceived it to be. The value in me doing this is that I am learning that my preconceptions can be wrong.

In the past, I didn't understand the concept of the two-way nature of social relationships; the give and take, the meaningless pleasantries that are exchanged. Therefore, I did not participate and was blighted both by the lack of knowledge of its existence and the lack of application – hence I am excluded on two counts from social interaction. More recently I have learned that with a simple amount of social effort, it is possible to receive acceptance, integration and a great deal in return. Although, it still appears to me as specious.

Sarah: Keith kind of gets it that in order to fit in, not get shouted at and have a girlfriend, he has to behave in certain ways. Naturally, however, he would choose to do exactly as he pleases. He has often expressed confusion at the concept that people do things that they don't want to do, in order to please others. This blows his mind! Why would anyone want to do such a thing? It makes no sense.

He has learned to say the right thing when he meets people, but on the whole he is awkward in company and much happier when we are alone together. During the time I have known him, his social AS traits have become less noticeable – he will now offer to buy someone a drink in a pub, which he would not have done previously. In the past, he would also have gone into a shop and bought himself chocolate and eaten the lot without asking if I or my son would like any.

He has no clue how he is supposed to imagine how I feel because he is not me. This is due to a less developed sense of empathy that often accompanies AS. He often looks stunned that I appear to be asking him to perform some magic feat, but seems not to notice that I do it all the time. He says: how can I possibly know how someone else feels, as they are not me? He states that to attempt to predict someone's motivation without asking them has an arrogance to it.

Enjoyment of particular, narrow interests and activities

Keith: For me there is no one overriding interest other than all things technical. I have passing phases, like ovens at the moment (I want to purchase one and have researched the topic obsessively); the same applies for cameras and mountain bikes. I love maps. I'm a bit of a computer geek. The common factor across any subject which grasps my attention is the attention to detail which I require in order to understand. For example, when researching potential candidates for a new car purchase – which I would carry out with extensive thoroughness – I discovered that the Renault Clio Sport had, probably, the world's greatest power to weight to cost ratio – i.e. it was the cheapest, quickest car around. This met all my criteria and I bought one. Subsequently, I knew all of the technical specifications and details of this particular model. Once the pinnacle of interest has passed at around the time of purchase, all the acquired information is then superfluous and easily discarded. Thus, I have a multitude of brief, passing obsessive phases that are readily forgotten.

Sarah: I am grateful that Keith's interests are not as all-encompassing as they are for some people with AS, and I am aware that this can cause difficulties in a relationship when all of the individual's free time is taken up pursuing that activity. The partner has to either go along or remain alone. I would find that very hard to tolerate.

Keith obsessively exercises at times, cycling many miles after work each day. This seems to help his depression and he enjoys the physical exhaustion that it brings. Despite being considerably underweight, he is obsessed with putting on weight and getting fat. Tony Attwood (2006) notes that there is a tendency towards low body weight for those with AS. I find it odd that someone scientific and educated has such little understanding of what is healthy and sensible in terms of diet, nutrition and body function, and even when evidence is presented to him, he will ignore it if it goes against his strongly held beliefs about how he wants to look and be. Whether this is a result of spending too much time alone or a genuine obsession, I cannot say, but he does seem to know what kind of bizarre noises and contortions his body is capable of – I shall say no more! He loves photography and takes endless photos of things – his cup of tea, me, himself, stones, sand – and often many pictures of the same thing. He never deletes any of them, so has thousands on his computer. He is currently fixated with his house in France, hunting for aerial photos of it on the internet; he wants a Rayburn taken out to the house and spends a lot of time looking at cookers. He has bought a computerised thermometer which takes the temperature at his French house every 30 minutes of every day for a year and stores the data for analysing later. Fascinating!

Keith: My BMI (body mass index – considered as a reliable index of obesity) is classified as 'ideal'. Yet, as anyone will tell you I appear gaunt, and Sarah says I am 'considerably underweight'. I am not underweight and if I'm not careful I could easily slip into overweight. The driving motivator for this is occasionally meeting with some of my old school colleagues. I've seen what the ravages of alcohol, comfortable, middle-aged and sedentary living have done to them. I don't want that to happen to me. I've always been active and can't bear to be without it. There are added benefits of vigorous exercise, it brings to me peace of mind by curing the guilt of not doing it, plus it brings me an enormous rush of calm. Actually it suppresses everything other than the desire to exercise more!

Lack of variety in behaviours, unchanging routines and habitual behaviours

Keith: This is interesting. The words 'routine' and 'ritual' don't encompass the reality. It's not that comfort is found from repetition, rather that the adage 'If it ain't wrong, don't fix it' applies, massively. This is not a conscious decision; it's merely a response to finding something that works. I find this to be so for me, and this works for dressing, for eating, for routines of getting up in the morning – everything. 'Unchanging routines' doesn't offer any explanation of the motivation, which is that if I find a method that works, it reduces the load on me. I lack imagination, I'll find a solution to a requirement and stick with it – it could be anything from wearing the same type of clothing to cooking the same meals. Even though the clothes may not be the most flattering for me, and the meals may not be the most nutritional, I've found a set of parameters that work, for me, so I don't need to do anything else. This takes the strain from me to have to think about these things again. This can be modified by, say, special interest. I will vary my drive to work and travel a whole range of routes to explore the local countryside, but I have worn the same clothes to work for the last five years. The clothes do their job, they're reasonably presentable, warm and cover up the naughty bits.

Sarah: It seems to me that there is an overload issue for many people with AS. New situations cause stress which accumulates to a point of becoming overwhelmed. Perhaps by reverting to a known method of carrying out a task, the possibilities of unpredictability or uncertainty are reduced. Tony Attwood (2002) suggests that routines make life predictable and leaves no opportunities for change. For example, dressing in a precise order and wearing the same clothes removes the need for decision-making about what to wear or whether an item has been forgotten. This allows more capacity for coping with every other challenge that life presents. If this is applied to as many areas as possible, this eases the burden of stress on the individual. Keith seems to have fewer rituals than many people with AS I have met. I have read of families who are bound rigidly to the routines and schedules of the AS partner, who will insist on eating at set mealtimes and dictate which foods may be served. Keith is very flexible and has no need for this predictability. He has a dressing habit which seems to be the same everyday. Most of Keith's inflexible adherence is to thought patterns. Any new idea or concept can take months for him to encompass into his being before it can be acted upon. His personal hygiene is fastidiously clean – not a ritual as such, but something he attends to without fail. It's a matter of respect amongst other things, I think.

Repetitive physical mannerisms

Keith: I knuckle-crack, and have done since at least age eight. I sometimes sway, rhythmically, a carrier bag of shopping in each hand, and a small twisting motion results in a lovely rocking sensation. A while ago I would leg-shake, too – either a rocking foot from a crossed leg, or a tapping foot flat on the floor – but found this all too weird, so stopped it. I knew about the knuckle-cracking (which, according to everyone else in the world, produces an obscene sound), but didn't know that the swaying was an AS trait.

Sarah: Oh yes, he twists and rocks his whole body and cracks his joints. He also bangs the heel and thumb of his hand on the table when he is writing or thinking and taps the toe of his foot on the ground. He looks awkward in his body and in the world, both at the same time. He tends to swing his arms, rock and look like he has no skeleton, very much like a small child. He has a revolting habit of cracking all of the joints in his fingers, hands, arms and shoulders very loudly and regardless of where he is or who he is with. I have seen entire rooms shudder at this horrible sound. I have asked him whether he has ever seen anyone else do this in public and he says no. I asked him whether he thought that meant that it wasn't very socially acceptable to do it and he said: 'No, it just means that they are not as liberated as me.' He very much enjoys provoking reactions in people – his churlish streak, as he calls it. I have known others with AS who hum, make loud noises when eating, burp at random without apology, bang on the table when stressed or relaxed; and I have known others who have no visible 'stims' (self-stimulatory physical behaviours) at all.

Focus on details, rather than the big picture

Keith: I would have said no to this, except that recently Sarah pointed out to me that whether I knew about it or not (and probably not), on one occasion I spent an inordinate amount of time making a food whisk wobble in a swaying action. And, now I think about it, I am accused by a work colleague that when in a hire car I'm the person who presses all the buttons and flicks all the switches and looks in all the nooks and crannies.

Sarah: This is not noticeable to a great degree. He does like to fiddle and tinker with things. He is a great perfectionist and things have to be done well, often at great length. He loves gadgets, tools and strange devices that are expensive, tactile and aesthetically pleasing. In a more conceptual way, he finds it almost impossible to see the 'whole picture' with regard to how his behaviour may impact on any given situation. He seems to exist wholly in the present – the past is forgotten, the future cannot be imagined so every action is not connected to any other. I think this is why he finds it hard to understand how someone can remain upset about something which happened a long time ago – for him each event is separate and solitary and finished quickly.

A level of significant difficulty in one or more areas of life

Keith: Socially yes. I've already said I have no friends. I didn't have any personal relationships until an advanced age. Whether these could be said to be clinically significant is a mystery: I have a decent job, a car, a mortgage (a second house) – I am capable of functioning.

Sarah: I think that this does impair him socially. He has missed out on all of the interactions that children and adults have which allow them to measure the world and learn about how they fit into it. He suffers from very dark periods of depression and hopelessness, which is harmful to his mental health. His self-esteem and self-worth are very low due to lack of input and integration with other people. I think his career as a software engineer, although perfect for him, has been hindered by the fact that he cannot progress to a level where working with people or in a team would be required.

Sensory sensitivity

Sarah: Other areas which are seen to commonly affect people with AS are with regard to their sensory experience of the world: some people are over- or under-sensitive to physical sensations such as touch, taste, noise, etc. Some people feel overwhelmed and overloaded when presented with too much sensory information, which causes them to need to retreat or shutdown in some way. This can result in anger or frustration for some or anxiety and withdrawal for others depending on their coping strategy. This sensitivity is different in everyone; for some it is a huge problem but only in one sensory area, for others it is milder but across more than one sense. I recently met someone who was reticent to wash his clothes because he found such comfort in relaxation in smelling his own dirty socks! He was able to articulate the calmness and pleasure that this gave him. Keith is certainly affected to some degree. The worst environment for Keith is a fast food restaurant; noise, too many options, bright colours, people. Pubs or bars cause similar difficulties as it is hard for him to participate in conversations when he cannot hear what is being said. He has real problems determining voices from background noise. Chris Slater-Walker expresses a similar difficulty in *An Asperger Marriage* (2002).

Keith: This is real hard to quantify. Because I don't have much contextual understanding it's hard for me to pick up from partial conversations what someone is trying to say in any situation. Combined with my demand of precision, I find that any missed word in a sentence or question becomes prohibitive in my understanding of meaning. So, loud environments are very hard to contend with. Noises and smells can readily offend. The same awful smells are guaranteed to offend, but sounds are a lot more variable; at times I can listen to music until the volume control won't go up any more and sometimes I just can't bear it.

Sarah: Keith has a near obsessive repulsion of vinegar. His reaction to its presence in any food is extreme and it is clear that he is physically distressed by it. This reminds me of my mum who had a similar reaction to coffee and would gag and shriek if she were mistakenly given a cup instead of tea. This is not unusual in people with AS to have sensitivity to taste, smell and other senses. When I first saw him have a tantrum in a café, I felt annoyed that he was being such a drama queen but have since learned that it really is intolerable for him, much like being served with dog poo on your plate, I imagine. Vinegar will arrive on his plate in the form of dressing on a salad garnish when he has ordered a sandwich or by way of mayonnaise. His intolerance of the substance is heightened by his irritation and literal interpretation that he has been given something that (a) was not stated on the menu ('Where does it say that there will be salad on the side of my plate?') and (b) he did not ask for. To avoid this I tend to do the ordering and make it very clear that there must be no vinegar, no dressing and no mayo. I probably shouldn't do this and let him sort it for himself, but the stress for me is too much to have him stomping about and raving.

Keith: OK, my preferences are such that I dislike vinegar. One of the advantages of being a self-sufficient, functioning adult is the ability to select preferences and disregard the dislikes: as a child (we all know the story) we're told by our parents that we will not leave the table until our plate is clean, that the meal in front of us will be heated up again and again until we eat it. Now, I only want what I want. I feel affronted that a meal should arrive with something unspecified and also feel that the creep of garnishing into foods is insidious. For example, consider the foodstuffs served in airline meals that are all pre-prepared and do not accommodate individual tastes, why spoil a perfectly good cheese sandwich and render it useless with stinky muck? I know this reaction sounds extreme, especially over something so apparently trivial, but to me it's important that options are offered, and that I'm not rendered optionless.

Sarah: He also seems to have a narrow band of temperature tolerance and still has his electric blanket on in June. I feel like I am in an oven when I stay at his house. We have discussed the possibility of having a duvet where one half is thin and the other much thicker! He also has a blanket on his mattress and a hugely thick duvet all year round. Keith gets cold very easily, shivers and teeth chatters quite badly when it doesn't seem to feel that cold to others. He finds light touch uncomfortable and prefers deep pressure and firm touch; hence he enjoys the feeling of being squashed under a heavy duvet or carrying bags. I have known several people with AS who carry large bags or rucksacks with them at all times as they find pleasure in the weight. Sensitivity to touch is a recognised AS characteristic.

Another facet that I have noticed is that he is as likely to say that I smell nice as I look nice. When we met I did not wear perfume as I have always been clueless as to what to choose. Keith spent about a year sniffing and trying out perfumes to find 'my' scent, as he put it – it had to be exactly 'me'. For Christmas he presented me with his choice, which was Chanel. I thought this was a lovely thing to do, which he enjoyed researching. I suspect that the real motivation was in satisfying his own sensory needs by having the right scent for him, but whatever the reason, I didn't complain as I have never been allowed to run out since. Not all partners with AS will be so keen to buy perfume, but may have a preference for certain fabrics and textures, so may choose clothes or underwear instead! I am quite happy to encourage his enjoyment in particular senses if it means he buys me nice things!

Some people with AS that I have met report insomnia or only require a few hours sleep per night. I think Keith could sleep all day, every day if he was left to his own devices. Sleeping is a means of switching off and not having to interact any more when overloaded. He falls asleep anywhere and will lie on my wooden floor right across the room and snooze at any time of day or night. He also falls asleep in the toilet at work.

Keith: I am aware that I seem to be less able to tolerate a wide range of temperatures than others. It seems that my internal thermostat is set high with a narrow band of comfort. I find smells and scents very evocative. Certain smells transcend years for me in a way that no other stimulus does. I tend to smell most things that are presented to me. I always sniff my food before eating it – partly to detect the smell of vinegar and partly to ensure that what I'm getting is what I want. I find smell a satisfying and illuminating method of interacting with my surroundings.

Physical issues

Sarah: Having read some of the other relationship research (Aston 2003) and online messages from women, I understand that many couples have difficulties with their sexual relationships. For some this may be related to the difficulty with sensory sensitivity of the AS partner who may find being touched painful. For others it may be related to the ability of the AS partner to understand the different physical and emotional needs of another person. Whilst not wishing to go into detail, I feel it useful to add our own experience on this topic. Keith did not have a sexual relationship until less than ten years ago, has had a relatively small number of partners, and yet despite all of this is a most intuitive and confident lover. I have no idea where he learned it from! Sometimes it feels as though he is another person within the privacy and safety of the bedroom, he has no inhibitions and is not constrained by the confusing social world. I can't explain why this is, but it is a stark difference to the awkward, clumsy, nervous person who I often see. There is a great sense of calm about him at these times. The usual loss of attraction and interest over time has never happened for us, perhaps in part because we don't see each other every day.

Keith: This will sound horrible: The concept is easy; it's a matter of understanding that sex is a shared process, everyone wants to get the most out of it, and I find that that can be assured if I provide what is required. This applies to the satisfaction of emotional as well as physical needs. The actual mechanics are also easy, it's all a matter of action and response; response is generally immediate and not hard to interpret. It's a situation that provides me with enough information to function well in. If only people were just as responsive in social situations then the world would be a lot simpler place for me to exist in!

CHAPTER 3

Relationship Mk I – Who Is This Weirdo/Crazy Woman?

Marriages work out best...when a person with autism marries a (handicapped or) eccentric spouse. The two partners get together because they have similar interests, not because of physical attraction. They are attracted because their intellects work on the same wavelength.

Temple Grandin (1995, p.154)

Sarah

I met Keith via internet dating. We had emailed for about three months before meeting. I had seen two photos of him. One was quite flattering and I thought that he looked nice; the other made him look painfully thin, strangely angular with a tree appearing to grow out of his head and very boyish. The words in his profile were about him being barely lucid and in his own world, so I should have known. I recall that my emails to him were somewhat direct, making it painfully clear that if he was looking for a wife and kids, he was wasting his time. Perhaps that got me the job!

It was a rainy night in January. I had arrived at the restaurant first and was seated at a table towards the back, some distance from the door. I saw him walk in and I waved, the waiter pointed at me to show him where I was. Sadly, his glasses had steamed up and he couldn't see a thing, so he stood dazed and confused whilst I leapt up and down trying to make myself visible.

He told me lots about fish and underwater acoustics, which is his job. I was genuinely fascinated and impressed because this was all new stuff that I knew absolutely nothing about, and I like that in other people. I remember him saying that I asked good questions and him seeming happy that I was interested in his job, which he said most people found dull.

We ate pasta; he had gnocchi. I reached over, stuck my fingers into his food and picked out a piece of pasta. I sat it on the edge of his plate and told him that his gnocchi looked like little bottoms. Knowing what I know now about some people with AS being very particular about food, this could have been the end of a very short relationship!

We went to a pub afterwards for a drink and sat together on a sofa. His body language was such that he was leaning so far away from me that he looked like he was going to fall on the floor. I had no sense at all that he liked me. He gave me a kiss on the cheek when we parted, said he would like to see me again and that was that. I thought how refreshing it was that he stayed sober and hadn't made any advances and was gently courteous towards me, but I wasn't attracted to him. He was quiet, calm and definitely too sensible for me to fall for. I decided this was a 'good thing' as I had recently been involved in a number of short, unsuccessful relationships. I couldn't cope with the trauma involved in being obsessed or madly in love with someone, so spending a few nice evenings learning how to be treated nicely by this gentle, quiet man who couldn't hurt me because I wouldn't get emotionally involved would be just what I needed. I knew that I would find it uncomfortable to be with someone so respectful and polite as I wasn't used to it, but felt it would be a useful learning process for me. Maxine Aston (2003) mentions that many women in her research state that the gentleness and non-sexual nature of AS men was an important factor in initial attraction.

I thought Keith was some kind of Buddhist; he was so self-sufficient and didn't seem to need the social approval that most people do. He was happy walking and cycling alone and living a self-contained life. I was in awe of this and thought he was amazing. It took me some time to realise that this wasn't exactly a lifestyle choice, but the only way he could function. He had a good job, a flat and a nice car. These things, sadly, impressed me as my history had been with men who had had none of them. I didn't care for the money or the possessions, only his capability in being able to achieve these things – I had found someone normal, at last! He was nice, but I was never going to fall for him.

Keith was so shy and didn't seem like a sexually predatory male, so I figured it would take some months before he would pluck up the courage to make any moves. It would be weeks before he even kissed me, I reckoned. This all added to my gentle fantasy of being wooed with handholding and chaste kisses goodnight. It was what I wanted – to do something different. It would be sweet and innocent. I would do nothing to encourage or assist him; I would wait for him to be ready to make his advance. I knew that he hadn't had a great deal of experience with women and that I could easily have taken the lead, but I was playing the fairy princess for the first time in my life and was not going to make life easy for him.

To be totally honest, I wasn't entirely eager to sleep with him. His whole demeanour was one of a slightly nervous, gangly, teenage boy; and rather arrogantly, I had drawn the conclusion that sex would be a rather fumbling, inexperienced effort where I would be forced to assume the role of worldly-wise teacher and have to show him what to do. I didn't want to do that; I was being a princess! Hence I was quite happy for it to take as long as it took for him to find the nerve to seduce a demanding, noisy, nosy, strident (his word) woman who had been about a bit. It didn't take as long as I thought.

On our second date…I shall spare you the details but let's just say I couldn't have been more wrong. He initiated masterfully, I tell you, despite my pathetic chirrups of 'We should wait, it's too soon. You don't do this sort of thing'. Resistance was futile. My preconceptions were shattered, I was in genuine shock. He said: 'You thought that was going to be crap, didn't you?' I meekly nodded yes. He appeared so un-sexual on the surface, so inhibited and yet in this private situation had been passionate, confident; wild even. Perhaps this was my first taste of learning that what you see is not what you get with this man with AS, although neither of us knew what that was or what it meant at that time.

So Keith and I began to see each other most weekends; we live 50 miles apart so this has all that has ever been feasible. During the first few months it was clear that he liked me more than I did him, and I felt uncomfortable about this as he was so genuine and I wasn't used to such niceness. He used to bake me gingerbread and bring it in little carefully wrapped parcels, and once or twice he made ice cream for me. I was bemused and slightly suspicious of this effeminate loner who baked. He ate little more than biscuits and drank 20 or more cups of tea a day and wondered why he couldn't sleep. He was great company, always sober, kind, funny and innocent, and I loved spending time with him. He was always by himself, did nothing at weekends except solitary activities. He looked like a boy; his clothes, the way he carried himself and his reactions. He was nothing like any man I had ever known. I was intrigued, if nothing else.

It seemed as though he had lived in a bubble or was really like a visitor from another planet. He didn't know what things were. He had experienced so little. Time and time again, I would start to talk about something – food, films, places – and I would be aware of a blank stare coming my way. Ploughman's lunches, hummus, chick peas, avocados and chicken Kiev are a few of the things Keith had never even heard of, let alone tasted. I remember a conversation. It went along these lines:

S: That's a cherry tree in your garden. You'll have your own cherries in the summer. Do you like cherries?

K: I don't know.

S: Have you ever tasted a cherry?

K: No.

S: They're a bit like plums, smaller but a similar texture inside.

[Silence. Blank look.]

S: You've never eaten a plum, have you?

K: No.

[More silence.]

K: I'm scaring you now, aren't I?

At about five months into our relationship, after me remaining fairly detached and just enjoying the company and attention, I clearly remember sitting in his flat, looking at him and being struck by the realisation that I was afraid at the prospect of losing him and that I really did have feelings for him. I wonder if that was when our troubles started. As I became more emotionally attached, fearful of losing him and seeking reassurance, he became less able to meet those needs. When emotionally involved, I wasn't making these demands for things he unable to provide. I had initially thought Keith's lifestyle was a choice. I thought he had assertively chosen to be self-sufficient and unaffected by social norms. I was in awe of this and liked his independence. It took me some time to realise that this was not the case and that this was the only means he had to manage and cope with life.

We spent 18 months together in all the first time, punctuated by several break-ups, usually instigated by me in frustration at his apparent lack of care and concern for me and my feelings. To me he was useless when I was upset and I felt terrible and out of control. I would shout and cry and become hysterical.

I would try to tell him how hurt I felt and he would calmly stare at me emotionless. Gisela Slater-Walker (2002) notes a similar reaction from her husband, Chris, in times of conflict. It made my head spin to try and understand why this person was with me when he seemed to want so little from me or be willing to give me anything at all. I found him selfish and uncompromising, and felt he had ridiculously unrealistic notions about relationships and offered me no hope for any kind of future together. In fact, he told me that there was none; that he saw us as temporary and that he would categorically never live with me or move nearer to me. He would tell me plainly that he didn't want to see me that week; that once a week was enough for him to see me and he had no need for more. I didn't need a guarantee of a future but at least some hope that maybe there was one. I heard the word 'never' a lot. It was very final, without a sliver of hope, and yet large parts of our time together were so perfectly wonderful that I was completely hooked and confused as to why he didn't want more of this bliss that we shared. I couldn't understand why if he said he loved me, as he claimed, that he wouldn't want to see me more often and make a commitment.

These rejections tapped into my worst insecurities; he told me I was irrational, needy and over-sensitive, so I concluded that he must be right. I was illogical, hysterical and disturbed at times. My head spun with his supposed logic, which was totally irrational, and came up with conclusions that I could never comprehend. I thought that if I could be different in some way – lose some weight, cut my hair, be nice, not get upset – then it would be OK and he would love me enough to want to share his life with me. I felt like I was begging for scraps. I was afraid to ask if I could see him as I couldn't bear it if he said no. I became tearful and distraught almost every time we spoke on the phone, desperately seeking reassurance and words of affection, not realising that the greater my demands, the further away he pulled and the less likely he was to say or do anything that would appease me. He couldn't see that he played any part in my distress and in these conversations – I started them, therefore I was the cause. (Tony Attwood (2006) identifies this trait in children who attribute all responsibility for an event to the person who started it, regardless of their own part in it. Typically, he states, a child below nine years of age will rationalise behaviour in this way, and yet here was a man in his 30s of high intellect relating to me identically.) It was a very unexpectedly immature response, which I could barely justify. If I didn't get so emotionally fraught, there would be no problem – that was how he saw it. There was no recognition that his distance and 'coldness' (as I then understood it to be) were causing me great sadness. I now understand that this bears a resemblance to Cassandra Affective Disorder, a condition identified as being a possible consequence of having a relationship with someone with AS. I believed I was in fact beyond help and that no one could ever put up with me. I was destined to be alone and lucky that Keith was even willing to consider having me in his life as I was such a disaster.

Sometimes when I did find some self-esteem, I hated him or couldn't be bothered. He was friendless, boring, camp, skinny, selfish, didn't seem to give a shit about me and just plain weird. I could do better. I had a life, friends, flexibility; I could do anything. What the hell was I doing here? He had nothing to offer me. I was the only thing in his life, whilst he was only part of mine. It felt like an impenetrable puzzle; we were so happy when we were together, more in love than anyone I knew, and yet he seemed not to want to stop the separations which caused so much grief.

I had mentioned AS to him in the first year we had been together, a friend who works in disability education had spotted it in him. I had known that something was odd but didn't know what it was. It was a puzzle that I couldn't solve, despite various misguided attempts. He had at first dismissed it and then slowly conceded that it did fit his entire life history – the isolation, the bullying, the difficulty in social settings – but we certainly weren't fully aware of what it meant in terms of his ability to communicate emotionally during these 18 months. I was hurt; he thought I was mad. It wasn't working. We both seemed to be losing the will to continue. I could increasingly see that he was never going to be able to move the relationship forward, and I didn't want to settle for so little for the rest of my life.

Finally, after feeling fed up of what felt like a relationship based on sex and Sunday lunch, we mutually agreed to stop.

Keith

I first saw Sarah (or rather I didn't) through misty glasses. I'd had a day working on a raft on a reservoir all day. Just as we were leaving the site my co-worker fell into the icy, January water. So, before my trek to see Sarah I had to rescue him and make sure he was warm and dry and safely collected by his wife. I was a little late.

Sarah and I had been communicating for a while before meeting. I first encountered her on an internet-based dating site. Internet dating is the ideal medium: it allows pre-selection filtering, and, because in the early stages it mostly involves relatively anonymous forms of communication (email), the gaucheness (physical, spoken, appearance) isn't so pervasive in the eye (mind) of the recipient. This reduces the chances of being dismissed immediately.

I saw Sarah's smiling face, flowing, curly locks and funny words on the website and joined so as I could get in touch with her. A number of emails, text messages and telephone calls ensued. I was struck by just how spirited, incisive and witty Sarah was. She was clearly not a passive person and her like I had not encountered before. I find these traits attractive.

We arranged to meet, and when we did I thought her uninterested in me – would I have known if she was interested? That's the question. After dinner, she suggested we went for a drink somewhere. I couldn't understand why, I truly thought that to get away was all she wanted; it was what I wanted as she clearly wasn't attracted to me. For me, it seems pointless to pursue someone who does not have any interest. I would not allow myself to develop feelings for such a person. (**Sarah**: Being liked by a potential partner is noted as a major feature in initial attraction by men with AS in Maxine Aston's research in *Aspergers in Love* (2003)).

We met again (Sarah and I have slightly different recollections over this), and on this occasion I very much got the impression that Sarah was warming to me, and as she says, I'll spare you the details, but Sarah remembers me to be masterful and I remember more of a mutual scenario.

One thing that runs through my head about the public persona I am is to always 'leave some in reserve', to drip feed people information about myself. To be full-on with everyone all the time feels indiscriminate. Yet I know that by retaining that air of reserve reduces the chances of people being particularly enamoured with me. It provides me with a sense of self-satisfaction though, that no one really knows me. This might explain a lot of what Sarah has noted about my being overly private. For me, a lot of AS is about self-perception, and I understand that some people have a distorted self-image. I don't know how to portray anything about myself merely from my visual appearance or read non-verbal language from others. The only way of getting to know someone is by verbal communication and yet this information is something I actively withhold. This is a contradiction which I cannot answer.

Initially we went though a period where Sarah was relatively distant and sane. She was clever, intelligent, outspoken, brash, harsh and questioning. We could hang out together and enjoy ourselves. This suited me. I was very in love with her. Gradually, she developed into something that became demanding and shrieking. I couldn't understand why she would ask questions that were impossible for me to give her the answer in the way she was looking for, like: 'Do you ever see us living together?' It felt as though she would pick at subject after subject until she found something that would make her upset, to explore its depths until she became distraught and then turn upon me. I never felt able to not respond, she would ask questions (questions I suspect she knew would give her an answer she wouldn't want to hear) and I felt compelled to answer. In my very literal way, I assumed that she wanted one; an honest one.

It became ridiculous: we were due to visit family of hers who were preparing a meal for us. I said I would not eat what was being prepared (fish) and they offered to cook me an alternative. She became angry because I had eaten fish the previous day and not complained. She felt that I had been rude and deliberately put her family to unnecessary effort. She asked why I would do such a thing, and the only answer I could give was 'because I can'. My take on the situation was that I was an adult and I have the ability to choose for myself. This infuriated her. She wailed; I got confused. That was the last straw.

Sarah had suggested to me, via a friend, that AS was a possibility by way of explanation of my sometimes odd behaviour. As usual when hearing something that I disliked I metaphorically (well, almost physically) screwed up my eyes, stuck my fingers in my ears and said 'mermermermermer' in an attempt to make it go away; to not allow it to invade my thoughts. My initial response was that Sarah was a fanatical diagnoser of everything: she had already diagnosed me as both gay and anorexic. So, I ignored her. It didn't stop me being curious: I wasn't gay or anorexic, but it was possible I might be weird. So, eventually I did my own tentative research on the internet and found that the more I read, the more I could relate to: solitude, awkwardness, lacking understanding. It took the best part of two years for me to fully acknowledge and embrace the magnitude of this discovery.

I recall the first Christmas time that I had known Sarah. I emailed a fellow university course member and candidly mentioned to him I was considering some form of counselling, which had been suggested to me by Sarah. Later, the following year when Sarah and I weren't so close it occurred to me that no, I didn't need counselling, I just needed rid of Sarah. When the girl went away, so did my mental anguish about…well just about everything. This meant that when Sarah and I were together, I felt anguished about almost everything, even when things were good, because of her ceaseless probing.

I couldn't tolerate the incessant trouble-making, as I saw it. Saying I tried to stick with it isn't quite right, rather I ignored it. I ignored it but it didn't stop. I could ignore it no further.

CHAPTER 4

The End of the Beginning – Splitting Up

S: I'm sad that it's over, but I hope you're happy now.

K: I have no feelings for you whatsoever.

Keith

I couldn't continue to be around Sarah. Life felt all too fraught with her in it. My life didn't feel enhanced by her presence. I felt it was a huge release to be rid of her and I felt capable of entering another relationship immediately, such was the relief of being apart from her. I didn't go through all of the grieving that people generally go through at the end of relationships because of this relief. If I'd learned one thing from Sarah it was the knowledge of what I didn't want. I didn't want the apparently irrational arguments that, in my perception, were always initiated by Sarah.

Since speaking with Sarah about this more recently, I now understand that she was receiving mixed messages from me: on the one hand I claimed to be in love with her and on the other I was unfeeling, cruel and didn't appear to care about her at all. I was simply being myself in the only way I knew how to be with anyone: blunt, honest and self-interested. This made her feel neglected, ignored, criticised and worthless, yet confused that I professed to love her deeply. It wasn't my intention to harm or upset her (and never has been). I hoped that my declaration of love would illustrate to her that all my intentions were good. Throughout all of our fighting, I had absolutely no concept that it was because of a difference of understanding; I simply thought she was mad. Now I can see that we were speaking two different languages. How else could Sarah react?

Within a few weeks I had started to see someone new. This was someone who was pretty, and that was about it, no, she lived nearby too. We met at a time when I'd just about had my fill of the critical self-analysis that Sarah insisted upon. I needed something simple, less strenuous. Initially this worked well and there was no strain. I wasn't questioned, I was given a break; a relief from the constant requirement to justify myself. I felt that everything I knew was being undermined and criticised. Some of my irrational thinking was being brought to the fore and my conclusions challenged in a manner that I found unpleasant. I was glad to be out of it.

What became apparent after a while, though, was that with all the shrieking and grief that came with Sarah, there was also a process of self-reflection. It wasn't particularly directed: Sarah questioned everything that came out of my mouth and every choice I had made in my life. Her interference was extreme but did stimulate a form of self-awareness that had not existed before. There was no mutual reflection with this new person in my life. She and I never developed together; didn't learn anything about ourselves or each other. I missed having my actions and motivations questioned; the process of which had made me look at some of my own choices and behaviours.

At this stage of my AS learning, I was still clinging on for a hope of denial. Sarah had started the process; I'd looked into and rejected it. It did not go away though. There were some things that Sarah had said and I had since observed that were undeniable: my social isolation, selfishness, rather bleak approach to life and inability to truly connect with anyone. I was becoming increasingly aware that this new person was aware of my 'differences'. It was becoming a hindrance and I didn't know what to do about it. I knew I had some responsibility in this but was unable to figure out what I had done and what I needed to do to make it better. So, a stunting of movement, thought, aspiration and self crept in. I could feel myself being stupid around her, not stupid funny, but stupid dense. I wasn't out of contact with Sarah for any great period of time and noticed that the more confused I was with my relationship and myself, the more I spoke to Sarah.

The longer this new relationship continued, the more confined, misunderstood, miserable and unfulfilled I felt. It was as though I couldn't be me – I had to put on some show to hide me. I don't lay blame upon my chosen partner. She had no concept of what she was dealing with and neither had I. My own understanding of AS was low and I had no comprehension of my needs. She and I had to part. It was very difficult for me. How could I have got it all so wrong again, yet how could I stay and lose myself?

I began to investigate AS for myself. The more I read, the more it fitted. It explained so much about my life. I remember reading articles in floods of tears, especially the more personal accounts (rather than the research papers which were trying to provide explanation/cause rather than showing any real understanding). With knowledge came relief. I don't have a medical diagnosis of AS, just a self-diagnosis. I don't need a medical diagnosis to be satisfied. The knowledge that I am not guilty is enough. It tells me there's a reason for how I think; it's not an excuse, but a reason.

Throughout all of this period I had relied upon Sarah. We had many telephone conversations and she had offered me more support and understanding than ever before. She too had learned about AS through her new job. This all made me feel like I had a true, solid, appreciative bond with her, the likes of which we had never had before.

Sarah

My initial feelings about splitting up with Keith were that it was a good thing; perhaps because we had parted several times before I didn't really believe that it was permanent. It was good to have some relief from the anxiety and frustration that I had felt in trying to understand this difficult man. It didn't take me long, however, to begin to regret what we had done and try to reconcile us, as I had successfully done before. Although I had been miserable for a fair part of the time, I didn't want to lose him for good. It became apparent that Keith had had enough. I made several pleas for his return, the last of which was met by an excruciatingly painful response. He said that I meant nothing to him; that he had no feelings whatsoever for me; that I should have no hope of him ever returning as he would not; his mind was made up and his head clear – all in his typically blunt formal style. My heart was broken. He had written off our year and a half together, said he could remember no good times and felt no pain or sadness about us no longer being together.

I remember feeling robbed of his acknowledgement that we had shared something special. We met once to exchange belongings about four weeks after we had parted. We went out for lunch in one of our usual haunts and Keith spent a fair part of the day sending text messages on his phone. This was a man with no friends; I knew he was seeing someone else. I was devastated. He showed no concern or emotion and appeared downright cruel. When I later asked him about this he said that he was seeing someone, that she lived nearby and that she was less hassle than I had been. He said that there wasn't the intellectual connection that he and I had but that it was just easier. He finally acknowledged that I had meant something to him, but that he was happier now. He said that his choices were 'constant drudgery' (with her) or 'depression and elation' (with me). He said he preferred the flat dullness, rather than the highs and lows of our time together. I genuinely wished him well, said that I hoped he was happy. I began to pick myself up and get on with life.

Within a few weeks of beginning his new relationship, Keith was sliding into depression. He was spending almost every evening and weekend with this person, but feeling out of place. He said that he felt he had lost himself. We had many phone calls which were highly traumatic and where he was in extreme distress and depression. He said he wanted to leave the relationship but seemed unable to believe that he had the right to. As he had got to know this person, he had realised that this wasn't what he wanted and that he had made a mistake. He felt that he wasn't allowed to change his mind and leave. It took several months before he felt able to do so. It was an exhausting and painful time to hear him being so distressed but knowing that he was spending his time with someone else. I was genuinely more concerned with his well-being than getting him back. It was becoming increasingly obvious that there was something very different about him and how he was coping with these experiences and I was unsure if I would be able to handle it and stay well myself. I knew I didn't want to rekindle what we had had previously, and yet we still seemed to have some kind of bond and understanding between us, which was hard to let go of. I think it was the general percep-tion of my friends that he was taking me for a ride and that I should tell him where to go, but I hoped and believed that this wasn't the case as I felt he hadn't the capacity for manipulation and deceit. It was a strange and unpleasant time.

During this time, I began my current job which put me into the field of AS. I received a lot of training and began to work with individuals and increase my own experience. I would tell Keith what I had learned during our lengthy phone calls and we had many discussions about how this applied to him. He slowly began to realise the impact that AS had had on his whole life up to this point. He did not tell his new partner about his growing suspicions of AS. Following the end of his relationship he withdrew for around four months into a deep and worrying depression where he saw no one and retreated totally. He seemed to have a great deal of trouble coming to terms with having 'got it wrong'. This seemed to be a kind of grieving process before 'coming out'. I know that since this period, he has positively revelled in his AS and avidly read and learned all he can about it.

During Keith's withdrawal, I spent a lot of time looking at myself and my behaviour. I also continued to learn about AS and was able to realise that just because Keith believed something to be true, it didn't mean that I had to agree. I wasn't necessarily 'over-emotional' as he had said; I was entitled to my feelings even if he couldn't understand them. I wasn't wrong. I learned that he was different and always would be, and that any attempt to change him would be futile and wrong. I realised that if I wanted to be with him, it would have to be more on his terms than mine, because I could bend more than he could. I learned that there would always be things that he found impossible and that my notions of a relationship and how someone shows their love may have to be redefined. No amount of effort or 'help' from me was going to turn him into someone else. I learned that he didn't need 'fixing' as he was fine exactly as he was. I remembered all of the wonderful things about him that I had liked.

I read a lot of online messages from women in the same situation. Many were as distraught as I had been, and yet they continued to stay and hope that things would improve. The stories were so familiar: claims of cruelty, coldness, controlling behaviour and being ignored – many more extreme that Keith's. Some had inappropriate friendships with other women; some had actually had affairs. All of it seemed explainable with my new understanding of AS, but not excusable. I wondered why these women stayed. It seemed to me that threatening to leave a man with AS was futile, because until you have actually gone he will be unable to imagine this scenario. Therefore he may not be motivated to change his behaviour on the basis that it might happen (but hasn't yet). The AS mind tends to be reactive rather than preventive and struggles with imaginary future concepts. I saw the evidence that women were unhappy and that their mental health often suffered as a result of these relationships. I questioned my own mental health for wanting to give it another go. Sometimes I still do.

I realised that I had spent my time with Keith in fear of his rejection, which seemed cruel and hurtful. I learned that none of this was personal or intentional; it was just his way of articulating his thoughts or viewing the world. There was never – not once – any deliberate attempt to be hurtful or callous. He had been frightened and confused by my emotional, erratic outbursts and had no idea what he was supposed to do. I had focused all my energy on helping him – finding jobs, counsellors, information – suggesting ways of behaving, improvements and changes, when there was nothing wrong with him in the first place.

I decided to change all of that and make myself my priority. I just stopped doing it, simple as that. When I caught myself not being myself or getting into 'helping mode', I stopped. I stopped feeling that Keith not wanting to live with me was a sign that I wasn't good enough – he had never lived with anybody, so it was hardly personal to me. I also started to stop the self-pity and be honest about whether I really wanted to live with him. I realised that perhaps I wasn't so sure; I had just enjoyed being the victim. I realised that whether Keith was in my life or not, I was fine and would continue to be so. I began to make plans for my own future, regardless of whether he was in it. I made sure that I told him what I wanted and what I would and would not accept, rather than waiting to be disappointed that he had failed to read my mind again. At that point, when I had stopped being needy, insecure and in constant need of reassurance; when I had made it clear to him what was required without confusion; when I just got on with my own life; that was when he decided he did want to be in it.

As far as Keith is concerned, he and I never ended; as he says: 'You were always with me.' He could not understand the hurt I felt and the fallout of that difficult time, which I can still feel. He feels that the fact that he is here now demonstrates his love. He focuses on what is real and current, he finds it pointless that I harbour hurt from the past.

CHAPTER 5

Relationship Mk II – Not So Weird/Crazy After All

Like bookends, we have learned to support each other when the stuff in the middle pushes us apart.

Lianne Holliday Willey, *Pretending to Be Normal* (1999, p.91)

Starting again

Sarah: The rest of this book is a collection of what we now know to be true and how we are now able to view what we have in a far more positive light. These are observations, loosely grouped about what and why Keith does what he does and how we now deal with this. Most of these observations are mine, commented on by Keith. I cannot reiterate enough how important this discovery and acceptance of AS has been for us. Without it there is absolutely no doubt that he would have written me off as an over-emotional troublemaker, whilst I would have discarded him as a heartless freak.

I thought about all of the people I know and, without making any allowances for AS, I can honestly say that Keith and I are as happy, respectful and appreciative of each other as anyone else I know; whether together for a few months or more than 20 years. Everyone has problems. Many people find it hard to meet someone, and relationships seem impossibly hard to sustain. For the majority, separation and divorce are commonplace. Does it make it harder if your partner has AS? I don't know. Perhaps it just makes it different. It may be easy to believe that without AS all would be well, but from speaking to friends and noting the rising divorce rate, that is certainly not the case – it would just be something else that caused problems: money, kids, stress, drinking etc. – AS is only one part of the equation in any partnership.

After being officially apart for around 10 months, although remaining in regular contact, we have slowly re-built a new relationship which is substantially different to the old one. Much of the background remains the same – living 50 miles apart, seeing each other at weekends, family commitments – but I, in particular, have learned to view things differently and not become upset and feel rejected as I did before.

Keith: After my retreat following the breakdown of my previous relationship, Sarah and I began to spend the odd day together. I can't identify there being a singular moment of thinking that she was the one for me. It was, and is, a gradual building process; from that comes the realisation that I don't really want to spend time with anyone else and that I doubt my ability to manage a relationship with anyone else anyway. She simply gets me.

Sarah: We always had good times together but these were interspersed with tears, anger and break-ups in the past due to confusion and bewilderment. I can honestly say that those days are gone. We communicate better and make the effort to work out what the other person needs. He is a lot more willing to compromise than before – I think he now knows that both parties need to feel that they are getting what they want. I think he is more appreciative of me now. It has been a revelation for us to be having such a different experience together.

We now spend more time together than we ever did, have holidays booked months in advance and plans for a life together in the distant future. The changes we have made have an increasingly beneficial effect: the happier I am because he is making the efforts I need, the more he feels he is doing a good job, which in turn makes him want to do more nice things…and so on.

Keith: One of the results of this improved communication is that I feel more amenable to spending more time with Sarah than before. It feels as though fewer demands are made upon me that I am unable to fulfil. This in turn allows me to be more giving, caring and loving. The culmination of all this is that all my needs are being met, and it's an environment that I thoroughly enjoy and want to continue enjoying.

Sarah: I spent a long time shouting, blaming, crying and being completely confused as to why this man who claimed to love me could be so callous and cold. Then slowly I realised that he wasn't being so; that reaction was my labelling of his behaviour. To be callous and cold requires an agenda; a deliberate desire to be unkind. I cannot say that is the case with Keith. He never means to be unkind. He simply didn't know. He had no idea what he was supposed to say or do. How could I blame someone for not knowing the rules of the game? When I came from the viewpoint that he was mean and I was mistreated, nothing changed. When I reframed the picture to show that he was just seeing the world his way and that I was misunderstanding him, things improved. I can't speak for all AS partners in this, and I am aware that some behave in ways that are more difficult to tolerate, but I wonder if underneath it all lies fear – of rejection, of getting it wrong, of being alone, of being imperfect.

Keith: When Sarah's needs are met, her anxiety and demands are extremely low. I am learning what is required to keep her happy. The benefit of keeping Sarah happy is that she interacts with me in a sane, calm, joyous, loving, caring, respectful, understanding and appreciative manner. Perhaps the greatest thing I have been able to take on board in terms of our relationship is that it only takes a little effort to keep her satisfied. For instance, Sarah told me that small, regular correspondence (phone calls, emails, text messages), albeit trivial according to me, can readily maintain a feeling of care and love in Sarah's mind. I struggle with this concept, as this type of contact, which she reciprocates, has little emotional impact on me, when it clearly does for her. I am amazed at what a difference it makes and how well it works. Simple things keep Sarah happy. I apply this to lots of areas where I feel I am underperforming and try to ensure that I can balance the giving element of the relationship. It is surprisingly easy. I just didn't know that that was all that was required before it was explained to me. There is now a complete absence of shrieking, which stems from an improved ability from me to listen rather than to be closed to any perceived criticism of myself.

Effort and attention

Sarah: Keith has always been the most adoringly attentive partner. I am not aware that this level of care is an AS trait, or even a male trait, according to my friends! From early on in our relationship he began to send me lovely cards with beautiful, simple words written inside – usually just a very few carefully chosen words. This continues to this day, and this is something that is very special to me.

Keith: I like cards, images and the emotions they evoke. It could be a photograph of a landscape; it could simply be a card with a star placed on it. They express emotion. I know I couldn't always say the 'right' thing and know that a token is longer-lasting and is a tangible, touchable thing that can be unearthed and found again, unlike fleeting words.

Sarah: He has always been very courteous to a degree which I have rarely seen in someone of our generation. He opens the car door, waits for me to get in and then closes it for me, he holds my coat up for me to slip my arms through, he always carries my things – bags, coat, shopping. I found this uncomfortable and a bit odd to begin with, having always been a stridently independent woman, and I would laugh and squirm when he did it. Now I am used to it but at no time do I take this for granted. It is a very lovely, sweet part of him that I hope never disappears.

Keith: I have mixed emotions about the opening doors thing! Whilst I know that in the times of equal opportunity it could be interpreted as condescending to be pleasant and courteous, I also know to receive such treatment is a treat, a sign that someone thinks and cares – plus I do enjoy the response from Sarah about something that requires so little effort from me. She is always appreciative and thanks me, and I feel as a result of my constant attention it helps contribute to and maintains, if not her interest in me, then her tolerance of me!

Sarah: He runs to get tissues if I am crying, has knelt on the floor in a bar to put a plaster on my foot (unasked), takes my glasses off and cleans them for me if he sees they are dirty. His attention and devotion are almost childlike in their innocence and are without any agenda or desire for reciprocation. Keith says he likes to be needed and have a role, that he feels superfluous without a purpose for being somewhere. The more he is able to do for me, the happier he is. He sees this as fair and reasonable and seems happy to have been able to contribute. He is always appreciative of me cooking dinner for him or making an effort for him in other ways. We enjoy sitting in the bath together. He always washes me, which feels such a tender and lovely thing to do. I asked him why he always insisted on doing this when at other times he does not always appear to make much effort. He said that he does it because he knows he won't fail and get it wrong – unlike many other things.

His childlike innocence allows me to stop being the responsible person I have had to be much of my life and lets me play. He never disapproves of me or tells me to stop behaving in certain ways. He does not see my behaviour as a reflection on him, and he would not dream of curtailing my freedom and would not wish his own to be limited.

Keith: I feel hindered and unable to do anything else other than wash up and help in minor ways in the house. I feel that Sarah has the raw deal because she makes decisions for both of us. She generally decides what to cook, so I try to do whatever I can for her. I fix her punctured bicycle tyres, design and maintain a website for her, buy her chocolates, wash her toes and legs and fingers and arms whilst in the bath. I'm capable of doing these things and can't get it wrong. To get it wrong would mean it shouldn't have been attempted in the first place (despite the fact that Sarah doesn't agree with this understanding and doesn't limit her appreciation to the things that I get right, but to all the things I attempt for her). This stems from a determined opinion in me that if something is to be done, then it has to be done right.

What else would she want me for, other than to do things? If I can't contribute in a tangible and beneficial way, then what is my role? This is a low self-esteem thing, I think. I have absolutely no idea why Sarah would want to be around me, so I do little things for her that I can get right and that I know make her feel cared for. Plus, I like Sarah doing lovely little things for me too; I feel cared for and thought about through it. She buys me the odd little gift (the latest is a miniature Lego model that looks like me, that is being taken on holiday and having its photograph taken in a multitude of places doing a multitude of activities, photos of which she sends me by mobile phone). I suppose that it's all another way of silently saying I care. It could be asked, is that the only thing I can do for her and do I honestly think that Sarah stays with me because I occasionally clean her glasses? I know there must be other reasons, and I know she tells me what they are, but I struggle to remember and to believe them. I have to express my love in the ways I know.

Sarah: I'm sure the challenge of unravelling his unfathomable nature is a huge part of the appeal for me. He doesn't make sense of things the way I do and this makes him fascinating. I imagine it would be like being with someone who speaks another language and has a different culture – life is a bigger journey of discovery when you cannot take these norms for granted. I am quite competitive and like to win, so giving up and admitting defeat would not sit easily with me!

I am a year older than Keith in age, but vastly more so in emotional experience. He has had so little practice, it's no wonder he is so upset and shaken by arguments and difficulties. Whereas I can quickly recover from a slight or a misunderstanding, it can take him days. I suspect this is a combination of lack of practice and of continually feeling that he can't get it right, being so hypersensitive. Sometimes I feel that my worldliness should give me some advantage over him, and sometimes it does. He is so much more 'pure' and unsullied than I am and makes me realise that too much emotion can be a bad thing. He will enquire in innocence and a puzzled desire to make sense of me and is sometimes very wise in his simplicity; perhaps my original notion of him as a Buddhist wasn't so far wrong! For all his insular, limited experience of life there are times when he forces me to look in that mirror and will bluntly (of course) tell me what he sees. The sharpness of his words make me wince, but once I have recovered, I realise he is usually spot on.

He says he has no idea why I am here. He feels he has nothing to offer. He is just going along for the ride and happy to be slipping under my radar until I realise that he is not worth it. I hate that he sees himself that way and feels unable to do anything that will change that. Keith feels that ours is sometimes an unequal partnership, he values my social skills and wider experience of the world more greatly than his calm stability, peculiar logic and eager practical support, I do not feel the same.

Keith: I can't help but feel that I get a lot more from our relationship than does Sarah. It means that I spend my time feeling indebted to her and always trying to do my best for her. There seem to be two elements to our relationship. One is the private aspect where we spend time together – this is the most equitable part, here we are smugly happy, do things for each other, explore, share and experience the world together, this is when I feel most like myself with another person. Then there is the aspect of our relationship when there are other people around. During this time I am aware I hide behind Sarah – almost physically as well as emotionally. The interesting point about this is that I don't need to, I can survive without her, yet I know that she is the better of the two of us at these times, so I let her shine!

Sarah: Keith is great with my son. He always has lots of time and energy when he arrives here on a Friday evening and I know he is quite over-whelmed from a week at work and just wants to hide in a corner, but he helps with homework, plays games, etc. I very much appreciate this effort on his part. He seems really to enjoy the freedom to be utterly foolish and silly and is a real clown. Perhaps he missed some of this childish frivolity when having such a miserable time at school. He engages totally and finds great joy in messing about with a football and making us laugh. He is very sensitive to putting my son's needs first, and has also been very careful to make sure that he is not put out or feels resentful of his presence. This was not always the case when we were first together, but was more out of lack of understanding rather than malice.

Keith: He is a great fellow. He's interested and interesting. This can only be attributable to the parenting he's received. Sarah has a wonderful relationship with him. She has engrained in him her intelligence and curiosity, her care and respect. This makes him very much like an adult yet has the curiosity that a lot of adults haven't, and he isn't complicated like adults are. It's easy to have a simple, uncomplicated friendship with him; it's the sort of relationship I'd like with everyone.

Sarah: I think one of the nicest and most valuable assets we have is that we have never taken each other for granted. This is partly due to that fact that we don't live together and so have less daily stress, but there must be more to it than that after three years. We are both very respectful and always remember to voice our appreciation.

Keith: For me, I'm sure that the distance and time apart contribute to this enjoyment of being together. It means that when we do get together it's because we want to, rather than we have to because we reside in the same house. This means I'm always pleased to see Sarah and am happy to show this – looking on the flip-side of this would be easy to say that shoved together 24/7 in the same house would mean we'd scratch each other's eyes out (I know this is a very AS way of looking at this situation). I'm not sure that that would be the case.

What our arrangement means for me is that I get the full range of acceptance: space, autonomy, appreciation, love, contact and shared enjoyment that I need. I have to add, though, that numerous discussions between the two of us on the subject of contact hint that this is not always entirely mutual, but I can only assume that Sarah gets enough of her needs met by this arrangement because she is still here.

Sarah: We are hugely affectionate and self-contained, almost to the point of excluding the rest of the world at times. He is a very attentive and loving person and likes to be physically very close – he holds my hand all the time and it sometimes feels that we are glued or magnetised together. I am aware that this is something that is often an issue for couples where one partner finds physical contact difficult, and I have experienced this in my own life with an ex-partner. I found this very hard to live with and often felt very rejected and hurt. I am grateful that this is not an issue with Keith.

Keith: The physical contact with Sarah is safe, and can't be misinterpreted; it's what two people do. But in most other situations I don't know the rules. (Strangely, don't want to know the rules, as the idea of touching a complete stranger feels quite bizarre. I have a French female acquaintance and in her part of the country there's an insistence on three pecks of the cheek when meeting people you know. I will oblige, but never feel comfortable or want to do it.) I like the physical contact, not in a definable sense, I just enjoy it. Also, what touching offers is the chance to be close without needing to articulate it. Surely not everything has to be spoken about and analysed to death. Just a held hand or a spoon in the night says a lot.

Sarah: We are very playful and happy; generally laughing and messing about. We have a lot of motivation to do nice things together – bike rides and picnics after work, buying our favourite chocolate, going for walks and having lunch. I remember once when in a shopping centre and upon seeing the escalators Keith said that he had always wondered what it would be like to run up the down escalator. I said 'Go on then', so off he ran and flung himself up the escalator, almost wrenching his arm out of its socket in the process. He seemed gleeful that he had been given permission to do what he had always pondered. In this, I suppose we are partners in crime as I clearly have little regard for social approval either and actively encourage his quirkiness and individuality.

Keith: With regard to the escalator and similar urges that I have: I know that some of the things I want to do, but shouldn't because I have a sense aren't socially acceptable, suddenly become available to me when encouraged (or at least not discouraged) by Sarah and take on a sense of possibility because she's in the real world. Therefore if she can behave in such a way, it must be OK for me to do so, and my previous misgivings must have been wrong. I understand that Sarah is not strongly bound by petty rules or boundaries, yet is still non-AS, and socially included.

Sarah: All these sound nauseatingly simple pursuits, and that I suspect is the beauty of our relationship – we are simply happy to be together. We are like two peas in a pod, happier alone than with others. Keith has said that being with me is like being alone for him – no demands, no stress, no awkwardness, he can just be himself. That is such a lovely thing to say. I think that is something that he has not found very often in his life and I am happy to provide it. It is quite innocent and naïve, I suppose. We both find each other's intelligence very important and attractive, and the ability to toss ideas and concepts around is a vital factor. I love it when he tries to explain something scientific and complex to me, he is so serious and does his best to put on a teacher's voice to instruct me, usually getting hideously confused along the way and losing his train of thought, scribbling things out and starting again. I have generally switched off because I am unlikely ever to understand it anyway and am happy to let him waffle on and listen to his 'important' voice.

Keith: My job as a computer programmer requires me to think constantly, such that when out of work I tend not to! Sarah is a deep thinker and probably the brightest person I know. This is my main attraction to her. One of the strongest elements of Sarah's intellect is that she won't let go. If there's a subject to be spoken about (no matter how uncomfortable), then it will be spoken about. Whenever this happens initially I find it very uncomfortable. Eventually, when I get around to thinking, rather than reacting to what she says, it nearly always turns out to be stimulating. The initial suggestions of my AS, purchasing the house in France that I now own, my own future and countless other topics were all instigated by Sarah's persistence. However, this intensity doesn't stop our mutual enjoyment in pure and simple nonsense, which frankly is mostly initiated by Sarah. Blowing bubbles in the field whilst having a picnic is the most important thing in life at that moment it's happening. These are the playful parts of life that I've simply not known about or have been hidden by the twisted 'logic' of AS in seeing play as 'stupid', 'unproductive' or 'resulting in nothing' and so shouldn't be done. Sarah is bright enough to bring this stupidity to my life, to bring some enjoyment to me and to shatter the AS logic on this point.

Sarah: Keith has made an enormous difference to my own self-confidence. He has encouraged me to be myself. I have never had such support to achieve and be successful. I have not read much about this in other AS relationships, so perhaps this is not related to the condition, but part of Keith's personality. I am aware of couples where the AS partner finds the other partner's success a threat and will undermine them in order to maintain control. My life has changed enormously since meeting him. He listens to all of my ideas and miseries and somehow helps without having to do very much. He is so solid, reliable and consistently there. I cannot imagine a time in my life, whatever happens to us, when I wouldn't want to talk to him. He sometimes says that I have had an enormous impact on his life, but he cannot see that he has done anything for me. No matter how many times I tell him, he doesn't really believe it. It is interesting that Keith tries to do practical things for me to make him more tolerable, as he puts it. I asked him if me doing nice things for him made him more willing to be around me and made him feel loved. He said that it didn't; he would feel no different about me if I did nothing nice at all. My main quality is that I tolerate him, that's it. Emotional things are much simpler in his head. When I ask him how does he think he shows me he loves me, realising that his way of demonstrating this may be different to mine and I may be missing it, he says: 'I am here.' That's it. Having his presence is his indication. If he didn't want to be here, he wouldn't.

Keith: You're irreplaceable, darling!

I know that understanding, appreciation and support are very important. So, I try my best to be positive in all my relationships with people. Even when something critical has to be said, it has to be said with a beneficial slant. I know how it feels to be demotivated (or should I say criticised) and I don't like it.

I want for Sarah the best that she can be. I want her to be what she wants to be. I perhaps feel that I am more faulty than Sarah is and she is able to see those faults. She is able to accommodate them and help me to look at myself and my faults to a much greater degree than I am able to do to her. Thus it feels unequal in terms of what I receive compared to what I give. I know that she wouldn't do that without a huge amount of love. I feel that one is only worth as much as one gives and, by that logic, because

I don't have as much to give Sarah as she has to offer me, I feel undeserving of the love she gives me.

Sarah: He says he doesn't miss me because I am always with him. He says he keeps his distance emotionally and remains detached so that he doesn't feel the pain of us being apart. Throughout the time we have known each other, whether together, apart or with someone else, Keith has always said he carries me with him all the time. It doesn't seem to matter to him whether we are in the same room or even the same country, he has me there. I believe that if we didn't see each other for years he could maintain the same degree of love for me when I would have lost interest and wandered off due to lack of contact. For me, being with a person and sharing experiences is what matters and I could not maintain that level of love and investment with too little contact.

Keith: It's true that my feelings would probably not change even if I never saw Sarah again. She has had such an impact upon me that it would be impossible for me to forget the magnitude of that impact. That's why she's always with me. To know that I've known her is very important. If we didn't continue to see each other, it wouldn't devastate me because we have spent time together, had shared experiences and at least had something. I like the continuation of being with Sarah but if it ended, I would have no choice other than to deal with it and get on with my life.

Sarah: For Keith, it sometimes seems like a fantasy to love someone but not have to go through the difficulties of actually sharing a life with them. For me, I want the real thing, warts and all. I don't expect him to be attentive at all times; I would be happy for him to come home after work and snooze on the sofa all evening as I appreciate the amount of energy it takes for him to negotiate the outside world. I don't expect him always to be in a good mood – that's just life and being human. He doesn't get this at all. I feel that the standards he has set himself on how he must be are restrictive and unrealistic. He feels he has to be great all of the time – he doesn't seem to have noticed that I don't set myself such standards!

Keith: I don't want warts; I want things to be as close to perfect as possible. I would rather have all or nothing. I share more of myself with Sarah than I do with anyone else. Maybe this is not to the degree that she would require, but to me I feel that I am making a huge commitment to her because I spend the amount of the time with her that I do. And yes, I would probably be sad, lonely and doing nothing if I wasn't, but that is a genuinely viable alternative to spending time with Sarah.

Acceptance

Sarah: I would not have considered re-starting a relationship with Keith had he not acknowledged AS in himself and recognised his contribution to our earlier difficulties. There would have been no point. I would have been banging my head against a wall trying to get him to see my point of view when he was not capable of doing so to a great extent. The fact that he is now aware that he finds this hard to do, at least allows him to see that I am not necessarily 'mad'. Maxine Aston clearly states in her research: 'There can be little hope for these relationships if the man does not become aware and accept he has a problem' (Aston 2003, p.150). That is not to say that he is 'wrong' but he does need to acknowledge that his way is not the only way, as much as I need to acknowledge that there are some things that I need to do differently or be aware of. Maxine again says: 'Awareness of the partner with AS is an essential ingredient if the relationship is to survive on a level that is not abusive or fraught with problems' (Aston 2003, p.152). She also concludes that continued denial will most likely lead to continued problems and often the breakdown of the relationship.

Keith: It's been a revelation! The hours of researching and re-researching on the internet were an emotional time for me. To see the words of other people saying virtually what I was thinking suddenly made this very real. It would have been futile to deny it. Sarah was the instigator of this thought process and it was with her I discussed a lot of my findings. Throughout this time I was becoming aware that she too was learning how this affects my thinking. The more I discussed this with her, the more apparent it became that I could relate to her on a personal level in all areas, not just about AS. I had no knowledge of AS in any relationship prior to Sarah. They all failed for one reason or another. I was always aware that there was something unfathomable about how I interacted with people on a number of levels. It could be an issue with communication: for much of the time I found myself lost and unable to understand what was required but aware that what I was saying wasn't what was expected or hoped for. On a social level, I have never been able to match anyone else. I know that I find group scenarios very difficult to cope with and would avoid them, much to my partners' irritation. Practically, what I found – and still find – is that in the presence of another person I tend to abdicate all my responsibility for fear of doing something that is misinterpreted, so can find myself almost completely paralysed. On an emotional level, I didn't know how to respond. What is becoming apparent to me is that not only do I have to be aware of the restrictions that AS imposes upon me, but my partner has to be aware of these too.

Through meeting Sarah, experiencing short-lived, unsatisfactory relationships and understanding and accepting that I might have AS, I can now sum up in a single word what I need in all my relationships with all people: 'acceptance', acceptance for the difference that AS has given me. For someone to be able to do this requires a lot of work: self-acceptance, understanding, accommodation, empathy, forgiveness, intelligence and open-mindedness.

Nowadays, Sarah does all this. She makes the burden of living in this world easier. I need to know that someone understands; that someone gets it. Around Sarah I am more like who I am in private than I am with any other person.

Sarah: Acceptance is Keith's definition of love. In the past I tried to change, whinge, cajole, force and persuade him to be what I would like him to be, and this caused him huge stress. Our recognition that we both need to learn about each other has changed the state of our relationship. It seems to me, in my limited experience, that all too often individuals with AS have been led to believe that they are the ones who are doing it wrong and need to fit in with the rest of us. They have been receiving that message throughout their entire lives. I do my best to do the fitting in for Keith and give him the freedom to be whatever he wants to be.

He says I am my own worst enemy as I let him be himself and don't place too many demands upon him. I could place ultimatums on him to do what I want, but I have to decide whether I prefer to have some of him, none of him, or all of him but under duress. I figure that if he wants to be here, then he will. I have to take this relationship for what it is and not for the potential that it might have if he could make a number of changes. If I don't like him for what he is and what he's got to offer, I should go and find someone else rather than give him a hard time for not being what I want. Ultimately I want Keith to be with me because he wants to, because it is pleasant and easy. Accepting him means he is happy and lovely to be around. I also want to be happy myself, and I love being with him when he is relaxed. So, we both win. If I were constantly being pushed out of my comfort zone in order to be with him, I would leave, so how can I expect him to do it for me? It wouldn't be a good relationship.

Keith: What I need is simple acceptance of me, for me. I feel that Sarah doesn't demand or expect any more of me than I'm able to give and this is just perfect (completely selfish, but just perfect). Being allowed to be myself doesn't give me licence to behave atrociously. What it does do is allow my loving, caring sides to flourish, because I have been accepted for who I am and not been asked to expand or be something I'm not. In previous relationships, it seemed to me that I was being deliberately provoked. This just resulted in me reverting to a defensive and almost offensive mode of behaviour: if my character isn't good enough for you, then why are you bothering with me? Don't expect me to be something I'm not. To a degree I'm a martyr to myself on this score, not because I expect people to understand me, but because I expect them to accommodate me; and when they don't, I'm not necessarily able to tell them so. This leads to an accumulation of resentment, which either results in me becoming depressed or leaving, or both.

I once tried to part company from Sarah, and have found that no one can provide the acceptance that she can. It's been said previously that being with her is like being alone. She makes me feel comfortable by her understanding and her lack of revulsion at my inability to conform. She just allows me to be myself. She doesn't excuse me my responsibilities as a partner, but she knows my limitations are genuine and not an act of idleness or malice.

Sarah: As for his ability to accept me and my feelings, I don't think he can to the same degree that I can. He simply doesn't appear to have the capacity. He can appreciate in a theoretical sense that I have different reactions to him, but can he really believe that my views are valid and react with kindness and empathy? Most of the time, I don't think so. This means that continually I have to justify my right to think something different, which is exhausting and sometimes upsetting. This is unlikely to change to any great degree and has to be tolerated and worked with.

Keith: I now acknowledge that others have different perspectives to mine, but this does not necessarily mean that I understand them. I have tried to take on board that what Sarah says and feels may be credible. I have tried to believe that some things are important to Sarah even though they aren't to me and respect this difference. It is very difficult for me to do this.

Sarah: I think that our entire experience has made me appreciate the value of individual difference to a greater degree. Some of the differences between Keith and me are very stark, especially when dealing with the complexities and hassles of life in general and, in particular, social interaction of any kind. He finds this more stressful than I do. In these instances, the casual observer would say that he has the impairment and that I was quite able. Unfortunately, these types of event make up the majority of life, and he is judged on this basis. However, if the measure of ability were changed to encompass coping with practical emergencies, completing a task to perfection, financial stability or directness, it would be me who would be considered low-functioning. Just last week Keith has been on a training course for work which involved fighting fires in pitch blackness, rescuing bodies from the scene, leaping into a life raft from a three-metre diving board and leading a team of people to safety. I would struggle to do any of these things and am staggered that he can do this yet flap at choosing food in a supermarket or being in a pub. Keith and I get along because we are different and because we are similar. Our differences complement each other; our strengths lie in different places and fill in the gaps: he is great at many things that I am useless at and vice versa. Our similarities bind us: we both like a quiet life, have the same goals for the future and share enjoyment in the same activities. Too many differences would make us incompatible. Too many similarities would prevent us from learning from each other. The labelling of Keith as someone with AS has been useful to understand the theory behind his unusual thinking and behaviour, but beyond that it's just a matter of respecting another's perception of their world, label or no label.

Keith: I know that I am different, and in my own personal universe I am perfect. It is the weight of evidence and continual failure from my interactions with the outside world that tell me that I am far from it. The message I receive is that I am defective and deficient. For most of my life, I had no idea why this was the case, and it was this that caused me the anxiety rather than my 'defectiveness' itself. Since learning that AS may be the reason, I sometimes revel in that 'deficiency'. I understand that Sarah succeeds in areas that I don't and that a lot of the areas in which I am capable are not particularly useful in this society. I don't discredit Sarah for her lack of similarity to me, quite the contrary. I find her ability to cope with people, multi-task (shopping, cooking, organising), use her imagination and deal with stress breathtaking. I feel that our different skills are complementary and we work well together as a team. A while back, Sarah needed a website designing (which I had never done before and had no idea how to do) and I thought we could do it ourselves. Sarah provided the content and creative ideas and I brought my particular attention to detail and enjoyment of technical learning, which when combined ensured a pixel-perfect end product. This site has been commented on by many visitors with regard to its beauty and ease of use (www.houseinmorocco.com).

Solitude and withdrawal

Keith: It is part of my nature to require periods of solitude. My need to withdraw is not a reflection on Sarah; I would do it whatever my relationship status. I am grateful that Sarah understands this and allows me the freedom to go when I need to, even though she finds this hard.

Consequently, when given the option to escape, my need to do so is less. Having the choice freely available to me makes this the case.

When I spend time alone, Sarah wonders what I am doing. The truth is I do very little. I watch TV (and regret the time spent wasted watching TV). I do very little both physically and mentally. This time is not spent thinking or pondering: my head is empty. I am devoid of thoughts, and therefore, stress. It is like a shutdown of all extraneous processes. This downtime is vital for me to be able to cope with the rest of life around other people.

Negotiating life with another person means having to think about someone else all of the time. It means coming home from work and not being able to switch off. It is a continuation of the thinking day. Not that I find time spent with Sarah stressful, but it takes definite thought and energy and brain power to make sure that our times together are as great as they are. That does require concentration and effort. I can't neglect Sarah; I can neglect myself. My head spins and whirrs and feels over-loaded with the effort of maintaining that level of calmness and happiness. When I drive over to Sarah's on a Friday evening after a full week at work, I am conscious that I am not as relaxed as I am on Saturday or Sunday. I feel that I am not able to give everything I should to her as there has been such a drain on my head already. I get that when Sarah is at my house and I return home after a day of work. It's great to see her there, but I feel unable to give her the attention I should. Most of the time when I come home from work I just want to switch off and do nothing. When I am around Sarah I feel that to do nothing is not good enough – that is my own perception, not the message that I get from her. It feels like another, but different, day of work to make that effort for Sarah. By nature I am a very flat, almost melancholic person, and even though Sarah and I share jolly, happy times, which we both enjoy, it doesn't come naturally to me and it requires a bit of work. I don't regret having those times and putting that work in, but it is draining all the same.

Sarah: I also need time to be alone and quiet, but not to such a great extent as Keith. I, in common with many parents, juggle a job, looking after children, running a home, a second job, lots of other projects on the go, a relationship and a social life. I often find all this overwhelming and need to have time to do nothing, but I do generally cope. Keith has a job and a relationship. He can't manage any more than that and so has to keep much of his life empty just to refuel from what he does do. I don't have such a pressing need, so it is hard for me to understand why he does. Therefore it could be easy to take it personally when he doesn't want to see me. I know from what he tells me that it is vital to him, and I have to respect that. I continue to learn that it is not an escape from me that he requires. I do ask for additional reassurance or support when he needs to retreat and to know clearly that he is not upset with me.

Sometimes I feel rejected by his silence or perceived lack of commitment, but then I look to see what anyone else in his life is getting from him. I get pretty much all that he has to give. It may not be as much as I have to give, as I seem to be more able to spend time with people and cope with the stresses of life, but it's all he has. How can I ask for more than exists? It is not personal; he is not refusing to see me and then going and doing things with other people. It's not because he doesn't love me or that I'm not important; it's because he needs to be on his own. This realisation has helped me a lot. I am the main, and often only, person in his world. I get 100 per cent of his social energy quota. He doesn't get that of mine – I go to other places and see other people. Just because I can do more doesn't mean I have the right to set the benchmark at my level as opposed to his.

CHAPTER 6

Practicalities

S: I have some time off; we could spend a whole week together.

K: That's rather a long time.

Living together

Sarah: We are both terrified of living together. He fears lack of space and freedom. I fear having to be a buffer for him to the world and sacrificing my own freedom in order to keep things calm enough for him. I would struggle with being shut out when he needs space. I suspect he doesn't need as much space as he thinks but fears being trapped in a situation he can't escape from. He always seems to need a get-out clause, in many areas of his life. He is always so happy at my house, sometimes surrounded by people. He seems to quite enjoy the socialising even. Of course, many couples are married and do share homes together, so it is not by any means impossible for a man with AS to do this. We are fortunate that it is not necessary for us to live together. I believe that Keith would pass all responsibility for solo thought on to me and I would be expected to deal with everything. This seems to be reported often in AS marriages. Resentment builds and the love is lost. I feel sure that this would happen to us under current circumstances. I have been married and spent a long period of my adult life cohabiting and didn't always find it easy.

Keith: As I have always lived alone and in relatively modest accommodation, my perception is that I would very rapidly become stir-crazy living with someone else. I feel that I would have to behave and think, and therefore not be able to relax and be my true self. The time that Sarah and I spend together at the moment is as joyous as it is because it is of known, fixed length: I know when I will be returning home to solitude. I know how much energy I need for that time and that I will be able to go away and replenish afterwards. That is not to say that I don't enjoy the time with Sarah, and I wouldn't miss it for the world.

Sarah: Keith would like us to live together in France in ten years or so, although we currently have no intention of living together in England. I used to get very upset that he didn't want to live with me and said it would never happen. I felt that I couldn't continue the relationship with someone who didn't want to commit or move things forward in the conventional, expected way, as I saw it. I was seeing his refusal to live with me as a measure of his (lack of) love. This was not, and is not, the case – he lives with no one, so it's not personal. I then asked myself if I really wanted to live with him and found that I had several reservations myself. I imagine it may happen one day in the distant future, but for now I enjoy the best of him when he is here; because he knows he will be leaving again in a few days, he can tolerate more; and I enjoy my own time and space when he is not here. He can be quite tiring to be around and I need to be away from that for myself. I need to have time to socialise without worrying about him, to focus on my son and spend time on my own interests. For now this suits us both.

Keith: I do have this dream that we will go to France, it is a beautiful place and there is no one that I would rather share it with. She is my best friend. Bizarrely, the prospect of living in France with Sarah in a decade's time seems less impossible than living with her here in England, today. It may be that because it's so far away that, given time, some of the uncertainties and logistics would surely sort themselves out. The prospect of living with her here is tainted by me being overwhelmed with work and the necessities of life. I don't believe that I have the energy to adequately support another person on top of my own life. I don't feel I have enough left over to do a good enough job of being a partner.

Work

Sarah: Keith and I both have dreams of a simple life where we don't go to work daily and can do as we please. He doesn't like working with other people. He has had only two jobs. He says his previous colleague didn't like him. His current colleague is apparently just 'lazy and wrong'. Keith's job is his special interest – he doesn't want any job, but if he has to have one, this is it. I have asked and expected him to move jobs to be nearer to me without realising that this is not as easy for him as it would be for me. I am flexible enough to be able to do any job just to earn some money, but he would not be happy doing something which didn't suit him, involved team working or an unpredictable work environment.

Keith: I'm overwhelmed by having to work and dedicating my time to this activity that I feel disassociated from. It drains me completely and I feel unable to do anything else. I'm continually wishing away the working period of my life. Let me retire right now so as I can go and do the things I want, or rather not have to feel manacled to something that feels as though it completely controls my life. I occasionally hide in the toilet at work just to get an injection of solitude.

Work takes up a third of my days during the working week. This is not extraordinary and is no more than most working people. Yet the interruption it places upon my time is such an imposition that I find trying to arrange anything else for the remainder of my day difficult. It's so hard to manage my time with all these things in my head at the same time. Plus, I have such a work ethic (starting work when aged 14 and knowing that hard work and perseverance will be rewarded, eventually!) that I can't relax completely. It's not always on my mind but is always looming above me. The only time I have been completely myself in recent years is when pottering aimlessly in the warmth and sunshine at a house I own in the south of France.

This might be the moment to mention a pessimistic streak that I own. Just about everything I do is tainted by something, nothing is perfect, nothing can be enjoyed for the moment, for I know that sometime soon, something in the near future will come along and spoil it all: a work-free weekend is spoiled by the forthcoming working week, a holiday is spoiled by its impending end, life marred by death.

Socialising and social skills

Sarah: If one starts out with few social skills, one doesn't get access to the world in which to practise them. This is the key to the non-AS social world: we have been practising since birth. When Keith has accessed this world with his partial set of social tools, he has made a mistake and been excluded, hurt or had the feeling that he somehow got it wrong, therefore limiting his willingness or opportunity to practise more. He has no reference points of other people to check his behaviour or discuss what went wrong because he didn't have the skills, couldn't practise, couldn't get access to others (friends) to further back up and correct these original skills. This is what non-AS people do. If I go to a party and no one speaks to me, I consider that it could be for a number of reasons, not all of them being my fault. I could conclude that they were rude people, that I hadn't made an effort, that no one realised that I didn't know anyone, that, perhaps, I didn't look like I wanted to talk, etc. Keith will see only one perspective, as is the AS way, that it is his fault because he is innately un-likeable. I will get over this event quickly, perhaps by running through it with my friends to see what they think, seek their reassurance that I am an OK person and think what I might do next time. I may feel a bit down and upset for a day or so, but it will not affect my self-esteem. Keith will add this to his bank of evidence that he is a worthless person and accept it as an inevitable event. Socialising seems to be a common issue with many AS couples and we are no exception. We resolve this by not doing it often or me doing it alone.

Keith: Sarah is right in her theorising. It's all a matter of success and failure. The weight of evidence says that I am destined to fail, so I rarely bother. It will be ultimately fruitless anyway. I have been unaware precisely what it is that I am lacking or doing wrong; I just know that I can never get it right. Sometimes it's easier to exaggerate my unwelcome behaviour in order to accelerate the disappointment in others and get the whole thing over with more quickly. I can be deliberately provocative by gauging someone's reaction to me, taking the behaviour that causes the greatest reaction and repeating it to an exaggerated extent. It reduces the drawn-out agony of the inevitability of the social exchange: I know it will eventually lead to failure, so why not encourage the process? Even when I have successfully become close to someone there is a fear that at some point the real me will be 'discovered' and I will be abandoned again. In order to avoid the uncertainty of not knowing when this will happen (for sure it will happen), I have a tendency to sabotage potentially good friendships so that I can retain the control of deciding when it should end, rather than at the will of the other party. To allow something to take its natural course would lead to disappointment, which would be another blow and the reinforcement of my belief that participation is impossible for me.

What happens is that eventually it becomes such a part of you – being ignored, being excluded, feeling uncomfortable, not feeling that you have gained anything or contributed anything – that eventually it becomes normal and expected and is no longer worthy of consideration. It just is.

We had lunch with a couple of Sarah's friends and then on the way home bumped into others for coffee. Sarah asked me did I enjoy the experience. It was not unenjoyable. I have concerns that social gatherings don't give due respect to a lot of the topics that are discussed. Topics are covered lightly and trivially and people flit from one to another in a fleeting, random fashion. The depth to which topics are discussed means that they are hardly worth talking about because they are not probed to any great detail and I don't feel that anyone learns much. It seems to be a process rather than a matter of learning, the process being talking about random episodic topics. I don't know if I call myself an intense person, but I feel the purpose of conversation is information exchange. Whether that is the same as socialising, I don't know.

Sarah: During our socialising today, I have met a friend's new girlfriend and found out about her life, laughed quite a bit, learned that another friend may be going to work on a cruise ship, discussed several foreign countries, trips and holidays, learned that another friend has given up smoking, whether two people enjoyed a film that they saw, discussed Chinese food and Chinese horoscopes, property in Morocco and growing vegetables in France, and shared several jokes and lots of trivial meaningless banter. Same day; different perspective. I feel that there has been 'information exchange' (as Keith requires and felt there was none), but the information was with regard to people and their lives, rather than fact-based knowledge, which is what he seems to view as more important.

Keith does not smoke and rarely drinks. At times I have felt that he has sounded judgemental towards those who indulge, but he denies this. I have to say that I have never met anyone so unable to handle their drink. Less than half a glass of wine makes his head spin and he literally staggers. He puts his head on the table in restaurants and closes his eyes or lies down across the floor, wherever he happens to be. I cannot believe this is purely due to lack of practice. It seems to me to be an acute reaction to alcohol, which is perhaps linked to research which suggests that AS is a metabolic disorder and that people with AS may metabolise certain nutrients differently (Shattock *et al.* 1997). He also finds it impossible to distinguish the taste of one drink from another. A decent wine is wasted on Keith. He will neck it extremely quickly – because he doesn't know how to drink socially (he struggles to do anything 'socially') and wonder why he feels dizzy a few minutes later. I find it refreshing that he doesn't feel the need to conform to this social norm and will not yield to pressure from people encouraging him to drink. I very much like the fact that everything we do is sober. This may stem from me having been in relationships with people who drank to excess at times. There may be some link between alcoholism/substance misuse and autistic spectrum disorders (of which AS is one) whereby people use alcohol as a social lubricant to reduce their inhibitions and anxiety around interacting with people. Chris Slater-Walker notes in *An Asperger Marriage* (2002) that alcohol, in moderation, helps to 'loosen a few social inhibitions'. This surely applies to much of the population to some extent and perhaps explains the appeal of alcohol.

Keith: Sarah hasn't quite understood my take on other people's drinking habits. She thinks I care about what others do, I don't. It doesn't influence me, and I can't (and don't want to) influence it. I avoid recreational drugs, tobacco and alcohol, not for judgemental reasons but because I know that my black-and-white approach to most aspects of life makes me fearful when contemplating these. I don't know what would happen if I found I enjoyed it. Perhaps it would consume me? I would not want that to happen. I will have the occasional glass of wine (accounting for no more than a couple of bottles a year), when feeling in a reckless mood, but have no yearning to pop a bottle in the evening after returning from work, for relaxation purposes – therein lies a slippery slope. My intolerance to alcohol can only be attributed to a lack of indulgence: imagine your first foray, that's how it is for me every time I pick up a glass, my body is simply not accustomed to metabolising it.

Sarah: When we go out socially with my friends, which is not often as we both prefer to be on our own together, I try to give Keith as much information in advance about where we are going, who will be there and what it may be like. I always give him the option to leave early if he chooses, but I may not go home with him. He seems to enjoy socialising more than when I first met him, all of my friends know that he finds it tough and make sure that they make an effort to speak to him and include him. He says that he is fine as long as he can see me somewhere in the room. I don't have to be by his side but within sight. I'm not sure why this makes a difference to him.

Keith: I am now generally more at ease socialising with Sarah's friends because they are familiar to me. Just recently I met a whole bunch of people (friends of Sarah's) and I wasn't at all comfortable. Sarah did note that for at least some of the time I was sitting in a corner reading. It is comforting to know that Sarah is around, for with just a glance across a crowded room she can see and understand my discomfort, and that is enough. It doesn't need to be taken away; just to have her recognise that I'm not at ease is enough. Sarah is not only aware, she actually understands.

Sarah: I tend to tell people that he has AS in advance of meeting him, so they will not react negatively to him if he does something odd. I am not sure if I am doing the right thing by doing this. He recently met some people I knew for the first time. We were in my house, so on familiar territory, and he knew several other people in the room, yet he spent most of the time in the corner and moved rooms when it became too crowded. After he had left, they said that they thought he was great and 'not as bad as you made out' and not much different to me (!!). This infuriates me by the implication (imagined by me?) that I have invented or exaggerated this for some personal gain. I feel strongly that this negates his experience of life and the extent to which he struggles. Just because he has managed to hold it together socially for a couple of hours does not mean that AS does not cause him difficulties. He said that next time he would prefer not to come as he found it so stressful, so to be told that he's 'just a bit shy' makes me quite angry.

Keith: I feel that Sarah takes the reaction of others' quite personally and that their perception of me affects her more than it does me. I don't really care what people think, as I feel I can't control this: they will think what they think. I don't mind either way whether Sarah informs people in advance, whatever makes life easier for her. I know she does it for the best of reasons, but others' reactions are not always as she hopes.

Disclosure

Sarah: Keith came to a training weekend that I ran at work for potential volunteers who support people with AS. It was at the time when he was just starting to fully acknowledge his own AS, and I asked him if he would like to come and listen to part of my training about AS itself as he might learn something useful. Keith decided that he wanted to be honest and 'out' himself and contribute to the session if it would be useful to the trainees. Consequently, I couldn't shut him up and eventually he decided he would leave because he knew he would keep butting in. I was speechless to hear him confidently talking about his strange habits, thought processes and stims. I thought it must feel empowering for him to be able to be so open in a room of strangers who were making no negative judgements, only seeking to learn. He had a role and a reason to be there. He had control and knowledge that other people wanted. I felt proud of him for being willing to do it.

Keith: It was a fun exercise in human watching to see how people preconceive and if these opinions are changeable. This was a group of people who had volunteered to spend more time with people with AS and I wanted to observe their reaction to my presence.

Nowadays, it's become very hard for me to impress upon my work colleagues that I might be anything other than strange. This is the difficulty: I appear, act and communicate in an entirely atypical manner. People just take this as a range of behaviours individual to me, and when I try to explain that there is a condition that encompasses (in fact, controls) all of these peculiarities, it's dismissed as just another of my tales or yarns and me being weird again. I don't really care if people can't see AS in themselves. I would like it not to be dismissed in me, though.

Sarah has been with me through all of my personal discoveries relating to AS and that is very important to me. It's been a growing process for us both. To a degree, she is the only person who needs to know. No one else really matters. It is more important for me to acknowledge this for myself than to have the acceptance of insignificant others. After all, what do I care about what others think of me, so long as I can live with myself?

CHAPTER 7

Speaking Asperger as a Second Language

It could be said that the NT (non-AS) partner's sense of humour plays an essential part in keeping the relationship together.

Maxine Aston, *Aspergers in Love* (2003, p.24)

Literalness and pedantry

Sarah: Language and communication issues are recognised as facets of AS. This can affect people in different ways – some have excellent verbal skills but poor comprehension, others may have good understanding, but lack the ability to express themselves in words. The ability to express and interpret language, both verbal and non-verbal can be an issue for people with AS. In my limited experience there do seem to be 'classically' AS ways of phrasing concepts which span across age ranges and gender within people with the condition.

Keith, despite his obvious intelligence, is a slow reader. This is by no means necessarily the case with all of those with AS. His spoken language is formal and precise, giving the impression of great comprehension and intellect. His head becomes cluttered with overload of information quite quickly, and yet this does not come across in his diction – his speech is clear and concise. His written language, on the other hand, is confusing, and he writes exactly as he speaks and is not always able to get his message across clearly. This inconsistency in language is not unusual in AS. He has failed English Language O-level several times. He loves to play with language and makes language-based jokes and puns. If I send him an email with a subject title, he will reply with a rhyming one, regardless of whether it makes any sense or not.

He has an odd, literal, formal use of language. He can argue about the context in which a word is used and be very particular that it is used in its correct sense. This has happened to me so many times at work with other people with AS! It is endearing and funny, but I can see how it could make him appear aloof and different to others because he does not share the flexibility and informality of language. He says 'in perpetuity' instead of 'forever', 'ample' or 'sufficient' instead of 'enough' and 'amplitude' for 'volume'. I will stop here and let him explain that amplitude is not the same as volume!

Keith: No, amplitude is not the same as volume. Volume is one of those overloaded words: it has more than one meaning, one being a setting of that big round knob on your audio system and is unit-less; and the other being a measure of space – having units: length cubed. This is a perfect example of why precision in speech is an absolute necessity. I'm an engineer by training and ambiguity is heinous, it leads to misunderstanding and mistakes. I know I'll interject a conversation by having to clarify a point – I'm aware that this sometimes annoys, but I feel it's necessary to ensure I'm understanding the conversation as intended. Wouldn't anyone do that, and wouldn't any member of a conversation want to know their audience is following them?

Sarah: Keith's speech is pedantic and sounds strangely old-fashioned, camp and formal at times. In my opinion, there seems to be a non-macho quality to AS men. I have never met anyone who is overtly masculine in a testosterone-fuelled way. Even when he is obviously annoyed with me, his use of language makes me laugh. When our relationship ended, I had made a final plea by text for him to come back and work things out. I received the following response: 'Sarah, do not have hope for me to return to you for I shall not. My decision is made and my mind is clear…' On another occasion, when I had texted him something unknowingly cryptic: 'Your last message was partial, stuttering and unclear. Please desist in corresponding unless you can be more transparent in your communication.' He wasn't even cross with me then, it was just a standard exchange!

Keith can often sound critical and judgemental. There is an implication that he is being negative, which puts people's backs up and makes them hostile towards him. A woman I know with AS also expressed her feeling that she seems (unintentionally) to provoke extreme reactions in people and is easily socially excluded. I think this is due to people feeling confused and threatened by getting an unexpected, non-typical social response. Surely, this is where racism and homophobia stem from (involving other oft-misunderstood or excluded minority groups). Isn't it a fear of the unknown, a threat to one's status quo and firmly held beliefs about how people 'should' behave, because 'they're not like me'? I often feel that being AS must be like belonging to another culture with its own set of customs unacceptable to the resident population. It is ironic that people with AS can provoke anxiety through their non-conformity in the same manner that they suffer anxiety from the behaviour of others. Keith was surprised when I told him that he can antagonise and be perceived as provocative; he says that he is totally tolerant of other people's choices and has no feeling of judgement towards anyone. I try to point out or clarify when he is sounding this way so that he, we hope, won't get such negative reactions in future.

Keith: I have to take Sarah's word for this. I don't know why it should be that I annoy to such a degree. It could be the tone of voice, the word selection, the passion?! Sarah has said that the feedback she gets from people about me is that I do provoke but, because I never get this feedback directly, at the time, I never know it. It mostly passes without comment and so has no significance for me; therefore I never learn, because I'm never given the chance to. Learning is a feedback methodology: if you walk in front of a moving car you get hit – immediate consequences, you learn not to do it again. If I annoy, but am not told (i.e. no feedback) then I can't possibly learn. Recently I saw an article that used linguistics as a form of diagnosis of autistic spectrum disorders. The point that is being totally missed in all the comment on the use of language is that words are the representation of thoughts: it's not the use of language that's unconventional, it's the thought processes behind them.

I do recognise having antagonised, and can understand it still. It goes like this: there are some things in life that are truly significant, like avoiding foods with vinegar, and then there are really insignificant things, like revulsion at hearing knuckles go 'click'. This confuses me, I'm unable intuitively to understand any other perspective or appreciate that someone else can have feelings or reactions that differ from my own. The antagonism comes from me attempting to question those feelings, but the only way I know is to be provocative in my questioning and hence ultimately it just ends up with me annoying people!

Mind-reading and brutal honesty

Sarah: Once I asked Keith (stupidly) if I was the most beautiful woman he'd ever seen, he said, 'No.' That hurt. I know, I know, I should have known better! I felt that, although clearly not super-model material, surely I should be more beautiful than anyone else to him, if to no one else. The next day, I decided to try to unearth his thought process around this, purely as a learning exercise. I reassured Keith that this was an objective question and that I would not get upset and that I wanted the complete truth. I asked him how important it was on a scale of 1–10 (1 being not at all important, 10 being vitally important) that I was not the most beautiful woman he saw. He said, '1 or 2.' He said that I was by far the cleverest woman he'd ever met and that was more important. I asked him who, in his opinion, was very beautiful. He didn't know because he had never looked! That made things (slightly) better. I wondered why he hadn't padded his original answer out to say some of that. He said that wasn't what I asked: he had just answered the question asked and no more. On further reflection, I thought that if I was absolutely honest, then Keith is not the most physically attractive man I have ever seen either, although I would never have said that and would have 'lied' and said he was the most gorgeous creature I had ever seen so as not to hurt his feelings. He does not have the skills to realise what is required and play the game. Do I want him to lie? Quite often, yes, I do. Am I pretty? Does my bum look big? If I look at it like this, then yes, I do want lies. This is hard for the AS person to tell and comprehend. He doesn't know the rules, which are subtle, multi-layered and ever-changing. I cannot ask him to play a game that he doesn't have the rule book for. What I do know is that when he does pay me a compliment it is genuine and truly meant – not a social pleasantry. Maxine Aston (2003) gives an example where a woman's husband tells her that his main recollection of the first occasion they had slept together was that he had been disappointed at the size of her breasts! Asking these types of questions is potentially damaging to the self-confidence and should be approached with caution! Perhaps some AS partners learn quickly what is required of them and can play these games to some degree.

He asks me why I ask such self-destructive questions, when I clearly can't take the whole range of answers. He doesn't ask because he doesn't want to know the truth. If I ask, he assumes that I am tough enough to take the truth (including: yes, your bum is the size of a house). I always assumed that he didn't ask for reassurance because he was so self-assured and confident. I now know that this is not the case. This has changed my thoughts about this a lot.

Keith: I never offer these loaded opinions without prompting. If you can't face all the possible answers, then don't ask the question. I think there might be something else going on here, but just can't work it out. The whole issue of asking questions is surely a matter of knowledge transfer – I only ever ask a question when I want an honest answer, why else would I? Whether this is just a male/female communication issue I can't tell, but certainly not many males I encounter bother asking a question unless it's worth asking. By which I mean, to ask a question is to ask for advice, to ask a question is to want to know the answer, and presumably if someone has bothered to ask a genuine question they must want a genuine answer. How much more simple can it be? I am aware Sarah asks questions that are not the type of question I would ask. The trick I've learned is not just to answer them in a way that exemplifies I have understood the question, but to give the answer I need to give in the format that Sarah needs. This is not always successful and sometimes I forget to do it.

I do not seek reassurance from Sarah as I feel I need to have that degree of self-containment, and have no control over her behaviour anyway. Therefore I don't seek anything from her, she will give it or she will not. I can't live with that degree of uncertainty: to worry about whether things are OK with her, in the same way that she appears to do. It's too fluid, the options for finding something that you don't want to know are endless and so I ignore any thoughts of this type. I quell them and am completely able to do this successfully. It's not that they do not exist for me; it's just that I will not allow them any significance. I am not arrogant enough to believe that Sarah will always want to hang around me, and if she doesn't then it is a decision beyond my control anyway. Therefore there is no point in dwelling upon this or seeking reassurance that it won't occur.

Sarah: When asked a question, Keith will answer only that question and provide no further information because that is what I asked! He has no idea what information is required. I find this amazing that he cannot guess in the same way that I can at what the underlying implication or intention is. I suppose for him it is amazing that I have this mind-reading skill that can pick up on what is not said, where he is relying pretty much only on the words, rather than the tone or hint of the conversation. It must make the world a baffling place when it's filled with nuances that he is oblivious to.

Keith: My literal brain can't interpret what others want. I have a tough enough job managing myself, how can I be held responsible for others? If someone asks me a question, I can only assume that the question asked is the one that an answer is required for. How dare I be so presumptuous as to add some form of imaginary context? My understanding is that if people are tough enough to ask a question, then they are tough enough to face all the possible answers. I advocate plain speaking, but I also advocate discussion, I'm sure I don't always have the correct phraseology and don't pretend to know everything, so the only way of coming to a resolution is by discussion/conversation. I might not always give people a chance to do this, by the apparently enormously emotional response I can evoke through my lack of tact, but this relates to the feedback process mentioned earlier. I do remember in the distant past when asked questions about a subject that would seem completely unexpected, I would have to provide as much information about the subject as I possibly could, in the hope that I would at least cover the question asked. On reflection I'm sure the questionner would have been completely baffled!

Sarah: Keith has a great ability for being direct and blunt: 'I do not want to see you this week.' Others may soften the blow or make excuses. He does not. I have had to get used to this and remember that it is not meant as a rebuff, simply a statement. It still hurts to hear this said so apparently coldly. I think this straightforwardness is common across many people with AS and the source of many social misunderstandings when they are considered rude.

Keith: This is surely neutral? To say 'I don't want to see you' is without emotion. Telling Sarah I don't want to see her means I don't want to see anyone, not that I specifically don't want to see her. I have the right to choose, but I know that she would say this is me imposing my demands upon her by insisting things go my way – yet surely, to not meet up at the weekend is less demanding than to do so?

Detailed information and context

Sarah: Not long ago, I was showing Keith how to play Risk (a strategy board game). I became very aware of his need for extreme detail and clarity in my instructions. If I described one item in the game by two different words, e.g. 'territory' and 'country', he was lost and could not make the leap that these may be the same thing. This was the first time I had noticed this in the three years I have known him. I got a headache; my ten-year-old son, who had grasped the game in minutes, groaned, Keith stomped out and returned with chocolate sulkily saying it was a stupid game. I remembered that he had said people at work were vague and unhelpful. I said that perhaps people were giving the level of detail that most people were fine with and that it was he who required something unusually specific. He said that his colleague had once impatiently asked him if he had any skills at all after Keith had asked a question, the answer to which perhaps was very obvious to most people.

Keith: Ambiguity is the culprit here. In board games, which have strict defined rules, all terminology should be consistent. If suddenly an alternative word is used to describe a previously introduced concept, it would be wrong for me to assume it was the same thing. Just considering this concept for this paragraph has made my head hurt! The fact that Sarah thinks it's OK to use two different terms for one concept or object when instructing me, is just completely baffling.

Sarah: Keith also requires an enormous amount of information to be able to understand what is required of him. I sometimes expect to tell him quickly what needs doing and he will get on with it, but this is rarely the case. The tendency at these times is to give up and do it myself as it is often quicker, which is not really helpful to either of us: I get fed up; he feels useless. It staggers me how he can fail to grasp what I would see as a simple concept and not be able to improvise. Every painstaking detail must be laid out. I find it hard to keep my patience and am incredulous that it seems so impossible for him. This appears to be quite a common trait in my experience and explains the fear of being considered stupid that haunts many people. Slow processing and an inability to make assumptions are the root causes here.

Keith: Following on from my last point, the level of ambiguity increases to the point of paralysis when I am required to improvise because, actually, what I am being required to do here is to read someone else's mind. When people say 'Use your initiative', what they are really saying is 'I want something, but don't know what it is, you go do it for me'. How am I supposed to react?

The lack of instruction is staggering. How am I supposed to improvise and accomplish something that my instructor doesn't even understand themselves? If the purpose is to allow me to complete a task to my own criteria, this should be stated because I am capable of that. What I am not capable of is guessing someone else's criteria, which is not explicitly stated.

CHAPTER 8

The World According to Keith

K: I'm being weird again, aren't I?

Sharing

Sarah: This refers back to the diagnostic criteria (Chapter 2). Keith speaks to different members of his family several times a week and yet tells them little about his life. He didn't tell them that I existed for almost a year. I am puzzled to know what they do talk about as he doesn't lead a sociable or active life. He feels that their interest in him is prying and cannot see why they would be interested in knowing what he does. He has said that things become 'tainted' by people knowing about them. Having met them a couple of times, I imagine that they must be quite concerned about his private, lonely life. It did take me a year of convincing him that it was not weird that I should want to meet his parents. He had no concept of why I would be interested in them or them in me. Naturally, that wasn't the case and they seemed relieved to know that he was happy.

Keith: I love my family. Sometimes it feels they are all I have. Sometimes it feels they are not there at all. We are separated by about 200 miles and I get to see them a few times a year; it depresses me that I don't get to see them more often. My sister lives just a few miles from our parents and sees them most weeks. I want to know what they're up to, to lose touch with their lives would be devastating. So, they (each one individually) will do the talking and I will do the questioning, with 'hmms', 'yesses' and 'whys' along the way. In terms of reciprocation, I don't feel I have a lot to tell in return, in truth there isn't a lot and I'm not proud of that. Hence it becomes easier not to bother. Also, the questions that come my way feel like an intrusion, and I get a sense that my relationship with Sarah is tainted by sharing private things with my family, and even merely by them knowing about and meeting her. What I do in my days has nothing to do with them…yet this is the sharing of their lives I yearn for.

Sarah: Keith doesn't see the interconnectedness of people and life. He compartmentalises me, his family and work into different boxes. He did this with regard to me meeting his family. At first he clearly stated that I would never meet his family as he could see no point and couldn't understand why I would want to. The subject was left as I felt deeply hurt by it but could see no option but to respect his wishes. Several months later, he invited me to come and visit them, and I have met them once since. Keith does not invite me to any family occasions, although I know they would like to see us both. Keith has arranged a forthcoming Christmas visit because 'I know how important it is to you to feel incorporated'. I love his way with words! He is very much integrated into my life, has met my family and friends and I like him to be part of things that I do. He is important to me and it feels natural to me to include him. I would like to be considered more in his plans, but I believe that his lack of doing so is not because I am being left out, more that he doesn't understand or even consider that it might be a nice thing to do.

Keith: I still don't get other people's desire to meet each other, as in Sarah and my family. I still don't feel the need. All I know is that to keep her happy, this is something I must permit to happen. I don't need it to, don't want it to, and don't get it either. It's something Sarah wants. Although I must admit that part of this is due to my own preconception of the event – I imagine that it will feel weird to have Sarah and my family together, although on the occasions that it has happened it has been fine. I simply don't understand the need or motivation in people to do this, and therefore naturally avoid it. I can't see why anyone would want to know anything about me, even though I like to know about them. I can understand how they would like to hear about others' achievements, but not mine. I am unsure whether this is low self-esteem – I am certainly the most important thing in my world and don't feel unworthy, yet I can't comprehend anyone's interest in my life.

Sarah: I feel that, despite the time we have known each other and the numerous, long and deep conversations we have, he remains elusive and unknown. I cannot make the assumptions that one could make about other people's motivations or likely behaviour. He will simply do what suits him. Luckily, this generally seems to take me into account, but I do wonder if one day he will just decide that this no longer serves him (as he so beautifully puts it) and disappear. He is baffled by people's interest in each other's doings. He considers this questioning out of interest as 'prying' and refuses to give much away. He could have an entire secret life as far as I know, as he reveals so little about himself. I have read discussions on this topic by other women with AS partners, so know I am not alone in this feeling. I think he would say that there is nothing to tell as he does nothing of interest. Perhaps there are no hidden depths. When Keith goes to visit his family, or when he stays with me, he switches his phone off. He compartmentalises people in his life and ensures any overlap is minimal. This makes him appear that he is hiding something, as that would be the usual reason for behaving in such a way. This is another example of me imposing an agenda on his behaviour that simply isn't there.

Keith: All the time that I have, I give to Sarah. There are no hidden depths and no secret life. I find it unnatural for her to feel that it is suspicious of me to switch my phone off. I give her 100 per cent of my attention. Why wouldn't I? I wouldn't expect anything less.

Logic?

Sarah: Keith said that he wanted to buy a house in France despite never having even been to France. A colleague at work had one and, as he had some equity in his flat, he would like one too. We went to France to have a look at some houses and see if it was as he thought. By the end of a five-day trip he had signed the paperwork for a house! Although this seemed very out of character for someone who lives such a limited and risk-free life, he said that it 'made sense' so he just did it. Now he has a new 'special interest' (the house) and something else to feel miserable about (not being there). When he decides that he wants something, he will ignore all reason, rational logic and pleas for patience and will just do as he pleases. He can be very single-minded and dismiss any amount of fact-based evidence in pursuit of his goal. I find this strange, as he is supposedly rational and a scientist. I think his logic is his own. He can explain the process that he is going through in his head, but some of the leaps and links he makes are really quite bizarre and draw conclusions that I would never come to in a million years. It's fascinating to hear. Interestingly, this logic does not apply to areas of his life which could seriously do with some action – like addressing his isolation and considerable periods of depression.

Keith: My AS head is dominated by logic. But as Sarah has experienced, this is not always a pure form of logic, it is wholly tainted by the whims of the AS brain. So, yes: if it makes sense, do it. In that instance it made complete sense. I know that I try to live my life by logic, devoid of emotion, rational – that's the only way that untainted conclusions can be drawn. In actual fact it turns out not to be logic at all, just my weird twisted values, completely spoiled by the limited range of thoughts by which I live my life. I truly do try to rationalise things, everything. This sometimes leads to perverse decision-making and probably explains a lot!

Detachment

Sarah: Whilst we were looking at houses in France, the estate agent accompanying us fell through a rotten attic floor in an isolated rural cottage. Keith was utterly capable and sorted, and possibly kept the man alive by talking to him to stop him drifting into unconsciousness. I felt distraught for days afterwards imagining how much worse things could have been. Keith said that those things I imagined didn't happen and I should stop dwelling. My imagination is not helpful in situations like this. His lack of imagination served him well. He moved on quickly, I was upset for long while.

Keith: I have received training on how to deal with people in physical crisis. I had no emotional attachment to the situation other than to keep the man safe. I thought that Sarah's reaction was emotionally unhealthy because she could, by way of her imagination, envisage endless horrific outcomes to any situation. I find that unproductive and an emotional waste.

Responsibility

Keith: Phew! Responsibility. This could be a whole book in itself – so, to keep it brief:

Ambitious, driven, focused? Well yes, to a degree. If things are going as I want I'm perfectly happy to leave it all to someone else and only take over when things become unbearable for me.

Actually, what happens is that when in the presence of another person the world takes on another level of complexity. I surrender just about every decision to whoever is there. Making choices and decisions that involve an element of shared responsibility is a nightmare, because I never know what anyone else is thinking or their motivations. I can never get it right, I can't second-guess. If I make a choice, it will inevitably be wrong, so it's simpler to abdicate all responsibility to whoever I'm with. Left to myself I can cope perfectly well, because I don't have to consider anyone else's perspective.

I am like a child; I have no concept of time and responsibility. It's not personal and not emotional. I tell Sarah: Don't take it personally, it never is.

As time goes by I'm getting to the root of this. Just recently I encountered a comment that the easiest way of 'curing' AS is to put the individual in a room and close the door behind them (Attwood 2006). Responsibility is a huge burden, to share it is unimaginably difficult: when around someone I revert to child mode and confer responsibility for all decisions to the other party (unless I am forced to take it on, for instance when working or recently when I took my father to France – his French was worse than mine, so I had to). Making a choice means the possibility of getting something wrong, annoying someone, or being blamed for something. For some reason, this is more horrific than making any kind of decision.

Sarah: I have tended to take over in places like restaurants when I know that ordering food is a bit stressful for him. I used to get annoyed about having to do this until Keith asked me how I thought he coped when I wasn't there, and I realised that I had just taken on the responsibility myself like a parent for a child and that he was perfectly able to do it himself. It is important, as a partner of someone who is basically self-interested (by design, rather than deliberate choice) to look after myself. He didn't ask for a martyr. If I want to run around after him and tend to his every need, he will certainly let me. If I can allow myself to see his perspective, then I am able to see why he allows me to do more than my share. I appreciate that once in this situation there will be a lot of resistance to attempts to change it, but I do feel that I have had to take some responsibility for enjoying the control as well as resenting the responsibility and workload.

Keith: I don't need anyone to run around after me. I can function by myself, it may be a weird form of functioning by any conventional description, yet I am alive, I have made it this far, and Sarah has even agreed to spend time with me. Just let me be me, and understand that whilst I'm still around things are still good. If someone is offering to do things for me, then I would be a fool to do it myself when I don't have to. If she didn't want to do it, then she wouldn't offer, would she? That's how I see it. Whilst I appreciate the help and effort that Sarah makes for me, I don't demand it. If I need advice, I am capable of asking for it. I prefer it when I am able to do things for myself and for Sarah. It gives me a greater sense of self-worth and confidence. To be continually told of how I may be improved or altered is perceived as a personal attack and is likely to be met with defensiveness or ignored.

Memory and organisation

Sarah: Keith has a poor short-term memory, as appears to be the case with some people with AS. It is very useful for me to remember this, as it has stopped me becoming furious with him on many occasions. I consciously have to make sure that I don't tell him too many things at once, and also make sure he has dates and arrangements in writing as he will completely forget. If he is occupied and I am trying to tell him something, there is no hope of it being retained. His organisational skills are also not too good. He takes forever to do anything. I accuse him of faffing, but he says: 'I do not faff; I prepare.' Everything must be done to perfection, even when it is not necessary to do so, and he takes an age. I admit that I am slap-dash and quick by comparison. I have learned just to get on with something else and not try to hurry him, as it doesn't work.

One weekend he came to see me and brought his camera complete with its battery and a spare, and both were flat – he had forgotten to charge them. The next weekend, he brought the camera but had left both batteries at home. He has an inability to think ahead and consider what he might need. When we visited Morocco, he took five fleeces and only a couple of T-shirts. He had not considered that it might be warm in North Africa. So, I made him a laminated packing list which told him exactly what he needed to pack, including how many of each item of clothing he would need depending on the length of the trip. This may seem patronising or pandering to him, but to me it is no different than Keith mending my bicycle puncture or fixing my computer – it is a skill which I find easy. It took me five minutes to make, in order to save him five days of stress every time he goes away from home.

Keith: The issue with memory and organising myself is one of loading, which typifies short-term memory limitations. If I am doing too many things or if I feel stressed at any one time, the likelihood of me remembering or doing anything effectively is severely reduced. It infuriates me to the point of distraction, and I find it immensely annoying and obstructive that I am unable to remember simple things. It is rare that a day passes by when I am fully prepared for everything, because I have usually forgotten something: a memory stick, mobile phone, lunch. My long-term, factual retention, like many others with AS, is excellent.

CHAPTER 9

Change, Certainty and Cantankerousness

S: Darling, why won't you marry me?

K: Because you might have an aberration and I might want to get rid of you. If we were married I would have to give you half my stuff, and I wouldn't want to do that.

Issues with change

Sarah: There have been several instances of Keith demonstrating the slow processing of new ideas that is often seen in people with AS. Typically, when introduced to a new thing, Keith will respond with a direct negative: no. He will argue quite strongly against the subject in question and reject it out of hand regardless of any positives presented to him. He will then quietly assimilate this information and at some later date suggest doing the thing in question as though it were all his own idea! I tend to sow a lot of seeds of ideas and then walk away and see what happens. If I nag at him to do something, he will do the opposite or do nothing. He can be infuriatingly stubborn and will not admit that he has been mistaken. Patience is required.

Keith: In order to be able to feel comfortable with something new that is suggested to me, I must assimilate the information into my being. I am unable to envisage what it would be like to experience what is being suggested to me; unable to imagine. It's quite a narrow world. Change can be tricky. When someone comes along and suggests a different solution, I'm forced to revisit and reconsider. This is the process that causes grief. This is why there's an instant 'No'. Consider it like this: someone suddenly tells you that your processes are flawed; it undermines everything you know about the subject. To rule out something outright that has been offered genuinely would be plain stupid. So, after a process of consideration I will either accept the idea/concept/notion or reject it if it's no better than I already have. If taken on board, then it will become subsumed into me as a part of life and doesn't need further comment. I know the lack of acknowledgement annoys Sarah. The only recognition she gets is to see that her ideas may have been adopted.

Sarah: When we first started to see each other, Keith took little effort with his clothes. I tried tactfully to hint at this in the most positive way possible and suggested he buy a pair of jeans that were more flattering than the ultra-tight pair that he always wore (he is very skinny). He became quite annoyed (perhaps rightfully so as he perceived criticism) and said that he had one pair of jeans which he had had for five years so why would he possibly need two pairs, that he was not some sad fashion victim and how could he justify spending £25 on such an item. I respected his right to dress as he chose and dropped the issue. Several months later, whilst out in town, I happened to mention that I had seen a jacket which I thought would look great on him. He asked me to show him, he tried it on, decided he liked it and bought it on the spot – it cost £50. Since then we have been on many shopping trips. He now loves buying new clothes and has become quite adventurous in his choices. He is also great to take shopping. He must be one of the few men who love clothes shopping for their partners and he always chooses things for me to try and likes to give his opinion. I have never heard him grumble about this, although if he says he is not in the mood for shopping, then we do something else.

Keith: This is akin to the change principle. I had rationalised the wearing of one pair of jeans until they were no longer wearable, only to be replaced another identical pair…because it worked, for me. It didn't work for Sarah, so she suggested something else. My huffing and puffing was merely the response of having that rationale quizzed. Once I'd gone away and thought about it a while, considered all the points that Sarah had made, in regard to the influence that clothes have upon appearance and therefore perception by others, and also the self-worth and satisfaction it can evoke, I could see that her ideas had merit, and decided to try them. Sometimes I, still, think the degrading practice of universal cover-all wearing and shaved heads allows a much truer understanding of a person to be gained. When you gauge a person by their incisiveness and individuality then appearance would not be a factor, but I do understand that appearance is an expression of individuality. So, when the mood takes me I rather enjoy clothes shopping and now own three pairs of jeans!

Certainty

Sarah: Keith has a need for certainty. He rarely says a straight 'Yes' – usually 'That might be possible' or 'I don't see why not' or 'No'. He says he cannot imagine life without me, would like to spend the rest of his life with me living in France, but at the same time cannot say for sure that I am the one for him. He cannot judge if what we have is OK. He said once that he needed to have two million relationships so he could truly know that this was the right one. He suspects that it is, but cannot be completely sure. Unfortunately for him, I am not willing to wait for him to do this so he can be certain! I explain that no one is ever entirely sure and that it doesn't really matter because you can leave if you decide that it's not right. Keith will not make any commitment until he is sure that it will work out. His standards are unreasonably high for himself and also for me. I wonder if he misses out on experiences because he is always waiting for a certainty and perfection that is impossible to find. He is very fearful of being hurt and being in a situation that he cannot cope with or cannot escape from; for example, living with someone.

Keith: I crave certainty, the only way I can ensure that is by being alone. When there are people involved, that is when the world becomes unpredictable, complicated, stressful and difficult. There is definitely a contradiction in this; yes, I do desire company (mostly) and this is to the detriment not only of privacy but also of certainty. Sarah uses the 'c' word an awful lot, commenting that she compromises most of the time when she is around me. What she hasn't got is that although I might want to be around her, doing so is a continual compromise for me. Not because of her in particular, rather the whole notion of sharing anything (time) with anyone is a compromise: a compromise of certainty; a compromise of freedom; a compromise of responsibility. That's the constant battle of contradictory influences raging in my head: want to be around people; can't stand being around people. The outcome is that it's hard to be certain of anything.

Certainty is important. Why would you bother with anything except if you were sure about it? Why would you waste your time with it? I'm not sure if what Sarah and I have is the best it could be. So, do I spend the rest of my days looking for something that could better it, or do I settle for what we have? I am aware that to strive for something different would result in losing Sarah, that the process would be unacceptable for her. I understand that completely. The only fact I am sure upon with our relationship is that I wouldn't want to lose what we have.

CHAPTER 10

Communication

S: When you do that it makes me feel that you don't care.

K: Yes, I can see that.

Silence.

S: That would have been a good time to tell me that you do care.

K: Oh, yes, sorry.

Empathy

Sarah: Let me put myself in his shoes. This is the skill of empathy that he by nature of his condition is said to lack. It is identified in tests developed by Simon Baron-Cohen (2003) to determine 'theory of mind' – whether a person is able to imagine a situation from another person's perspective. Those with autistic spectrum disorders are said to have a less well-developed theory of mind. This results in their outlook being more self-interested and apparently uncaring – the ability to 'care' or feel someone else's experience may be impaired. The person can only imagine their own experience, not someone else's. Because Keith has no desire for a bunch of flowers, he will find it impossible to comprehend that I might. So, I want him to take me out for dinner, buy me flowers and make some romantic effort.

I am asking him to do something perhaps because everyone else does it. He cannot see that everyone else does it, or if he can, why everyone else does it. So he is suspicious because he has no motivation or desire to do it. Yet I try to convince him to do things on this basis.

If I was asked to do something that I didn't want to do and could see no benefit in doing, would I do it? I suspect that I would not and would take some great amount of convincing. This person is not bound by following the herd and doing things because others do them. This is one of the things that I found so attractive in him and now it drives me mad! I think this is how it is. He simply doesn't know why he should do this stuff. He hears it and is aware on that level, but because there is no desire for him to have it, he can't see the point. So, it's hard for him really to believe that I would want it either. On top of this the sheer panic at making a mistake, having to make decisions, plan or organise something that I might hate may override any desire to do something wonderful. None of these romantic gestures would make him feel loved, so he can't see how it could possibly be such a big deal for me.

The best way to get what I want is just to tell him. If I want flowers, I ask for flowers; if he hasn't called me for a few days, I ask for more contact. Rather than feel bossed about, he is happy to know what to do as he seems unable to think of these things unaided. Of course, I would much prefer that I didn't have to ask, but not asking means no flowers and no calls!

Keith: Meaningless gestures and dead plants are not appropriate signs of my love. For me, being here, in this relationship, is the best indication and measure of my feelings for Sarah. I don't see why I should adhere to society's expectations as to how I demonstrate my feelings. Saying that, I can listen and I know that Sarah would not ask for something if she did not want it, so I do try to respond when I know what is required. If I do not know, I am unable to guess what I am supposed to do. I do not feel that this is demanding of her as I still have the choice not to respond. Mostly, I am pleased to know what I can do to make her happy.

Difficult discussions

Sarah: Keith believes himself to be good at communication, whereas I feel that this is only the case if he is in control of the subject matter, if it is something he is happy to discuss and the timing suits him. I think that most people are like this to some degree, but seem to be able to manage even when these conditions aren't present. I have read of women whose partners shut down and refuse to speak to them for days, and others who 'meltdown' and become extremely angry. I know that becoming very emotional is totally pointless, as this seems to make him withdraw from me even further, which is the worst thing he could do when I am upset. He also has a terrible short-term memory and forgets many things that I have told him about or asked him to do, which doesn't help.

Our disagreements take a standard form: I express that something is not how I would like it, he reacts badly. Generally, I try to use good communication skills and remain calm, reassuring him that he is not being criticised. I am not always able to do this. Keith takes any comment on his behaviour as a personal attack and becomes immediately defensive about the fact that I have raised an issue. The issue itself becomes irrelevant. I then justify my right to raise issues and we have an argument about that. Along the way I may say, 'What about my feelings?' and Keith will say, 'What about my feelings?' I try to get back to discussing the issue but he is too affronted by my mentioning it to consider that. My impression is that I come at Keith with a feather duster and he returns fire with a machine gun. I feel that it is him who turns a calm discussion into full-scale war by his sensitivity. It seems ironic that I am expected not to take things personally, because he tells me that they never are, and yet he is highly sensitive to any comment or request. I find this one of the most frustrating and depressing aspects of our relationship, as no matter how often we discuss it, it's clear that his view hasn't changed. Luckily it happens only rarely these days, but it's still a shock when it does. His responses can be very immature and impossible to reason with. Despite this, I know he tries very hard and he now knows that when I am upset I don't want to be left alone (as he does), I want to be held and listened to. He does do this at times, and it helps us to get over our disagreement much quicker than when he would refuse to speak to me and I would feel increasingly ignored and uncared for. I know that he finds this tough and appreciate his efforts a lot.

Keith: When within a relationship people communicate difficult stuff to each other it is inevitably about each other and that's why I become defensive, because if it's difficult then it's a moan and it's a moan about me and something I'm doing wrong. I'm never deliberately malicious or intentionally reprehensible. So, yes, the defensive claim is justified.

Justified on the grounds that I feel offended and when in this position I do withdraw, it's a simple protective reaction.

Sarah: Keith cannot understand why people argue or disagree at all. He has asked if I can tell him everything that is likely to bother me now so that we can get it out of the way and never disagree again. I say that it is impossible to know every thought that you or anyone else is going to have in the future, or every event that will happen in your life, so there will always be situations arising for which each of you may have a differing reaction. This is a ridiculously simplistic argument from me but I don't really know what to say. He is searching for certainties that I cannot give. The main evidence of my case being more realistic, which I tend not to point out to him, is that he and I have different views on lots of things, have far more disagreements than he would like, and yet he is still here!

Keith: It seems that no matter who I am involved with there are always arguments. I feel that if you love a person and accept them entirely, then this should exclude the need for argument. Why would you love someone whom you are going to argue with? I can't understand why these disagreements happen. Is it because I have AS or because people are inherently nasty to each other at times? By this I mean other people, not me, because I never start arguments.

Sarah: When Keith made the above statement about whomever he is involved with, there are always arguments, I pointed out that the common factor in all his relationships was him and that perhaps he was the problem. He said that no, that couldn't be right: he just went out with argumentative women!

In the past, Keith and I had a long history of arguing on the telephone, mainly because we were not together in person but wanted to be and so vented our frustration the only way we could when not in the same place. Keith's only solution to this was that we should never speak on the phone again. He could see no other solution at all. He couldn't consider that we could communicate in different ways, such as minimising phone calls to shorter times so we couldn't get into deep, heavy debates or any other alternative. We still phone each other but argue very rarely as we are happier generally and also are aware that this is a weak point for us.

Face-to-face communication is all that really works. I am aware that some people find this difficult and use emailing as a means to share difficult thoughts (Slater-Walker and Slater-Walker 2002). We have done this a lot in times of separation, but there is still misunderstanding due to our different use of language. Keith can still sound patronising, cold and pedantic by email!

Keith: I don't always know how what I've said is being interpreted. Sometimes the only way to establish this is by asking supplementary questions immediately after I've said what I've said in order to gauge if the right understanding has been made. This can be done over the phone, but not with email or text. We have gotten into hopeless difficulty through word usage using written communication methods.

Black-and-white thinking

Sarah: Keith has a rather black-and-white view that if things are not perfect then they must be awful. This is part of a trait referred to as 'monotropism' (Murray and Lesser 2006), which is a tunnel-visioned way of looking at the world and results in this kind of all-or-nothing viewpoint. The person constantly feels caught off guard and confused by a seemingly erratic and roller-coaster world. This applies to the most mundane of things. Keith has grown a beard, which was beginning to tickle his top lip. He said he was going to shave the whole thing off. I suggested that he trim his top lip to remove the annoying hairs but keep the beard. He had not considered this as an option! 'Beard' or 'no beard' were the only two possibilities in his mind. He literally cannot think of alternatives.

Keith: I seem able to cope a lot better if I have a binary opinion about everything: it's either one thing or the other. I either like something or I don't, I can do something or I can't, I can see a resolution or I can't. This way of thinking reduces the loading in my head: so long as I know how I feel about something then I may put it away out of my thoughts with no mind-consuming loose ends. It feels easier than to have a plethora of options and never knowing which one to take. In practice, I lose out on many things because I dismiss them through the inability to think about them any other way. Using the beard example: I know how to grow a beard – just don't shave. I know how to get rid of a beard – shave. But, I didn't know how to do the tidying and trimming and hadn't even considered it as an option. Not that I lack the intelligence, but my head could see only one option to resolve the tickly top lip, and that was to remove the whole thing.

To the outside observer it must seem that I have an extreme view of every subject. In actual fact, all I've done is to consider whether I like or dislike. The idea of using 1–10 scales discussed below allows me to reconsider, although I need some guidance to assist me in doing this.

Whilst working together on this book, Sarah is writing and asking Keith for his viewpoint on various AS-related topics.

S: Extreme black-and-white thinking. If something isn't great, then it must be awful, hard to consider lesser degrees in things.

K: Simple way of leading your life.

S: Yesterday when you had a headache, I asked you to scale the pain from 1 to 10 and you were able to do that. You said it was an 8.

K: Oh yes, you're right, I could. Generally I do see things in black and white. For example, food – I either like something totally or dislike it – there is no middle ground. You either will eat something or won't eat something. It's a binary state.

S: What about the cake we had yesterday when we were out? You ate it but you said you weren't too impressed. That doesn't sound like an 'eat or not eat' situation. So where would that be on a scale of 1 to 10?

K: About a 3 or a 4.

S: Not a 1 and not a 10. Your argument is flawed! I suggest that your inability to contemplate degrees lies in a difficulty to put feelings and thoughts into a scale of words. It's not that you do not feel the feelings but that you find it hard to link the physical feeling with a word which describes it. So that you couldn't describe being angry in a scale – irritated, furious, pissed off, cross, peeved, miffed, annoyed. You would be angry or not angry.

K: Yes, I agree. I don't think that I don't have the vocabulary. It's that the emotions are complex and hard to rank. They are all encompassing.

S: So, by giving you a scale that removes emotions, words and feelings – 1 to 10, you are able to rank those feelings without becoming confused. We could use this to find out all sorts of information about how you feel and also for you to understand the degree of my feelings.

K: That's amazing. This could be an invaluable means of communication.

S: This could work the other way round as well. I think that you do understand that there are degrees in feelings and moods but are unable to communicate them or understand when I try to communicate them. If I were to tell you that I was upset '8', you would find that easier to react to appropriately and appreciate than if I were to say that I was furious or cry and shout at you.

K: It would give me access to your feelings in a way I have never had before.

That's about as exciting as life gets for us!

Understanding intentions

Sarah: I no longer take anything he says or does personally. This is a vital component in our improved relationship. I have to believe the motivation behind the actions. They are not meant deliberately to hurt or neglect. Once I had grasped this – it took me around two years – I felt a huge weight lifted. I realised that none of his behaviour was because I wasn't good enough or wasn't trying hard enough. It was nothing to do with me at all. He wasn't not calling me because he didn't want to talk to me, he wasn't calling me because he didn't want to talk to anyone, or he didn't have anything to say, or he hadn't even considered the option of calling me.

Keith: I believe myself to be a good person. I believe in treating people the same way as I wish to be treated, which, of course, is well. Central to this is that I never intend to hurt, harm or be inappropriate. I never set out to be a bad person. So, when someone is offended or hurt or riled or upset or angered by my actions or words, it generates confusion for me. I simply don't understand how I can evoke such emotion in anyone. I try my best to be clear and plain (upon the basis that any question asked during a discussion is a genuine question warranting a genuine answer) and answer everything honestly. How can I be held responsible for the content of an answer if it's true? I never intend to harm.

Sarah: He asks me questions to clarify things in his own mind, but sometimes this can be hard to do because I have never been asked these questions before – most people seem intuitively to know the answers. For example, being asked why people in relationships have difficult times and disagreements is something that most people would just accept as being for an infinite number of reasons and circumstances. Being asked to explain a fundamental part of life leaves me struggling for words. I understand that Keith's need for answers is genuine, but I find that being the main or only source of this knowledge for him draining and exhausting. I suppose it is useful for us all to consider these issues.

Keith: Is it unreasonable to ask these questions? Is it unreasonable not to know these answers? It is mutually difficult: we think differently; although Sarah has a great ability to put herself in my head and seems to be able to anticipate most of my thinking, a lot better than I am able to do for her. It's rare now that I surprise her. These questions only arise in response to observations and discussions that I have with Sarah. Without this input, the opportunity to ponder these points wouldn't occur.

Sarah: Keith is extremely passive and finds it hard to comprehend that this may be contributing to my screaming fury at difficult times. He has said that I cause arguments because I start unpleasant conversations. He struggles to recognise that, from my perspective, his behaviour may have been so unreasonable that I had no choice but to voice my upset or remain silent and become increasingly resentful and angry. On many occasions I kept quiet, as I knew that speaking out would not improve anything. Unfortunately, the knock-on effect of this is that I stored up this irritation and hurt until it came out as a great explosion of anger triggered by some small event. Keith's perception was that I had hugely over-reacted to something insignificant and hadn't seen it coming. My perception was that I could stand no more. Keith says he needs to learn that his tone or words are misconstrued and his motives misunderstood, but that he can only do this at the time it happens, not at some time afterwards. I find it hard calmly to point out my grievance at the time, as I am usually so annoyed that shutting my mouth is the only way to prevent something horrible escaping! Despite this I know that Keith is right and that the only way he has any hope of being better received socially is to be told. So, we have agreed that I will try to do this in future. I pointed out that this may mean more small arguments, as I will be mentioning everything that annoys me at the time it happens instead of keeping quiet. Our method for this is to punch each other on the arm if either of us says or does something upsetting or inappropriate. This is immediate, tangible and doesn't involve confusing emotional words. It is an easily readable signal that something needs attention. It does sound strange but it works.

Keith: The learning process is a matter of exchange, if I get no instant feedback that whatever heinousness has just tripped from my tongue has caused huge offence, then I won't know. This has caused me some distress, for not only have I not intended to cause harm, and as far as I'm concerned I haven't (i.e. no instant feedback), but also, when this tirade of negativity occurs it appears completely unexpected, without warning and without reference.

Sarah: During our time apart, I was fortunate to attend some training through my work, run by Maxine Aston, an AS counsellor and author who has worked extensively with AS/non-AS couples. From her I learned to tell Keith how I feel when upset or angry – he cannot guess from my reactions. I tell him that it's not his fault – even though his behaviour may have caused my upset, it is usually not deliberate and therefore he is not to blame. He always assumes that he is, so is pleased to know that he is not. I tell him what I would like him to do – leave me alone, give me a hug, make me a cup of tea – although fantastic in a practical crisis, he is paralysed with not having a clue how to respond to emotional needs and is grateful to be told what is required. This really works for us.

Keith: It's so beneficial that Sarah can do this. I know it's unconventional, but is absolutely necessary. I feel that I was limited in the past from achieving a successful relationship by my inability to communicate successfully. If the visible signals were strong enough, I could tell that my partner was upset, otherwise perhaps not. Even ascertaining this, it would not help me to guess the cause. To have this spelled out to me allows me to provide the necessary/expected behavioural responses.

Demands

Sarah: Keith does not seem to feel jealous or insecure about what I am doing or who I am with and places no curtailments or demands upon me. I very much appreciate this. I remain close to my ex-husband and we go on holiday with our son together. I also have several male friends that I go out for the evening with. Keith never asks that I don't spend time with these men or restricts me in any way. I am very appreciative of this freedom, as I am aware that not all couples operate in this way. I am very open about what I am doing and who I am seeing so I have no secrets from Keith. I can't guarantee the same for him, as he is not always great at providing information that is reasonable. He feels that any request for information is prying and implies a lack of trust.

Keith feels that he makes no demands on me at all because he doesn't expect me to make any on him. I feel that he does make huge demands but more passively. He requires far less contact when we are apart than I do, so will sometimes not respond to messages left. I find this hurtful, annoying and downright rude. He struggles to see that by doing nothing he can cause upset. Things tend to be on Keith's terms much of the time because he cannot cover up when he is uncomfortable as easily as I can and is less able to adapt to unfamiliar situations. He also passively demands that I tolerate the lack of information he provides and separation he requires. Quite rightly, he would say that if I don't like it I can leave, but this leaves little room for compromise.

Keith: I have the sense that trust means not prying. I don't pry, interfere or demand anything of Sarah. Sarah says that my doing nothing in itself places demands upon her. I am baffled by this. The trust I offer is simple respect: she is an independent adult, does what she wants and should be allowed to do so without interference or imposition by me. I demand this back and wouldn't tolerate anything less. I make no direct demands on Sarah, I don't ask her to do anything for me, but it seems that simply by being me, the way I behave places my own set of impositions upon her. She doesn't understand that sometimes I wish to see no one, and that this isn't directed towards her, sometimes I don't wish to see anyone. Sometimes her emails and texts are so complete they don't demand a response from me, if she did want a response she would ask a question...surely?

I didn't impose anything upon her when we didn't know each other and I continue not to do so now. Sarah thinks that because now we do know each other, she has a weight of imposition put upon her. Clearly this is a subject I find very hard to comprehend.

Sarah: Sometimes I have to assert a need for myself that he doesn't like. I try to remain calm and speak clearly. I tell him what the issue is and what I expect him to do. If it is something that is non-negotiable, I stick to my guns and tell him what he is doing is not acceptable. I cannot assume that he knows basic social or relationship rules that I would take for granted. I find it is necessary explicitly to state these so we both understand what is being said. Generally, he will claim that I am unreasonable and have no right to tell him what to do. His conviction and outrage are sometimes strong and it feels hard to defend my right, but I have to do so at times. I let him withdraw, process and consider things, and often he will begrudgingly agree at a later time. Remaining calm and not expecting an immediate answer makes a big difference.

Keith: Everyone is entitled to express their opinions, but I do not have to agree with them. When confronted with difficult communication, I may see this as critical of me and react defensively and withdraw. I find it difficult to respond on the spot to new information, especially if it is presented to me in an emotional manner. If I am allowed to go away and reflect upon what has been said, I am more likely to be able to consider it rationally. If I am persistently asked for a response before I have processed the information, I am unable to do this.

CHAPTER 11

Pay-offs, Sad Days and Thoughts

I sometimes have to explain to a person with Asperger Syndrome that as much as blood trickling from a wound indicates physical pain, tears trickling down a face can indicate emotional pain...

Tony Attwood, *The Complete Guide to Asperger's Syndrome*
(2006, p.149)

What follows is a summary of some things that work for us, the pay-offs in being in an AS relationship, and also an acknowledgement to the odd times when it all gets too much.

Pay-offs

Keith: Sarah has turned out to be the best friend I've had. She allows me to relate. I know this may sound like a huge responsibility, but I don't need much, I don't need her to do it all for me, I simply need to know that I'm not alone. That knowledge is enough to alleviate my head from the frustration of there never being anyone who can/does understand me. It is not the case that I crave the attention, more that I need to know that there has been at least one person during my lifetime I can relate to. The majority of my time is not spent with Sarah; I am not forever at her garment's hem, to know that she is in the world is good enough, to spend time with her is a bonus. When we are with other people, I know that I can be tiring; needing to know the social intricacies of what to her is normal life. Perhaps this is why we get along so well when it's just the two of us, I can relate to Sarah without needing constant explanation.

All of this does tend to an interesting question: exactly what do I need from a relationship and what am I doing with Sarah? There is love, there is care, there is learning, growing and bettering. From Sarah I get a taste of life. So, is that it, is that all? I suppose this question is applicable to any relationship. I have learned that to ensure Sarah continues to provide what I need, so as she remains calm, loving, caring and giving I have to be responsive to her requirements of me. I accommodate and compromise. Are all my actions so selfish, so calculated to assure I get what I want? Ask yourself what are your own motivations? Do only I have the gall to say it?

Sarah: There are a number of positive aspects of being with Keith which may be as a direct result of him having AS. These are the pay-offs. This is why I want to spend my life with this man. It is too easy to focus on the difficulties and concessions he requires, but he also ticks more boxes for me than any other man I've known. It is not a matter of having to 'put up with him'; I consider his AS to be a big part of what attracts me to him.

- High intelligence. He is very intellectually capable and loves to engage in good conversations and discussions.

- Utterly solid and reliable. If he says he will be there, he will be there. He has never let me down.

- No hidden agendas or deceit. What you see is what you get. Although he appears complex, he is less so than most people. I make things complicated by adding assumptions that do not exist for him.

- Honest, completely, even when you don't want him to be! Sometimes it is necessary to ensure I ask the right questions in order to get all the information as he doesn't know what is required.

- Not bound by social rules. He doesn't do things because other people do them. He follows his own path. It is liberating and encouraging.

- Sense of humour. His way with language enables him to make complex linguistic jokes and his (unintentional) pedantic use of words makes me laugh.

- Self-awareness. I think I have forced him to become so, but it has been necessary for him to like himself.

- Playful and childlike. He is capable of being very silly and will perform in order to make me laugh.

- Non-macho. Like most AS men, there is a gentleness about him. He doesn't try to prove his manliness with bravado.

- Doesn't really drink, smoke or take any recreational drugs. He looks after himself.

- Financially sensible. It's just nice to know that he won't ask to borrow money!

- Gives 100 per cent of what he has to me and this relationship.

- No demands and no restrictions upon me. I can go and do as I please.

- Incapable of jealousy. This is an emotion which makes no sense to him. I will either be with him or not, and there is no point in worrying about it.

- Hugely supportive and wants the best for me.

- Great at practical help, fixing things.

- Good to talk things through with – he doesn't let emotions impede his thinking process. He helps me cut out the excess.

- Gentlemanly, courteous, polite and respectful, always.

- Quite simply, he is the loveliest man I have ever met.

Sad days

Sarah: It would be dishonest to not come clean about the sad days too – the times when I wish things were different. I'm sure Keith has these days too, although he says he doesn't. I think that in his black-and-white universe, if he felt like this, he would simply leave, whereas I appreciate that less good bits are inevitable and all part of the package of any relationship. These moments are rare these days. This is the sad stuff that I suppose is mainly specific to AS, although not exclusively.

- At times I feel sad about the inequality. I would like a partner who can anticipate some of my needs, who can see the point in random romantic gestures and visits when I am in hospital (is this too much to ask?!).

- I wish we could go to social events and I could feel protected and looked after by my partner, to hear him introducing me to friends, to have him command a group or people with his witty repartee, to see him dance. I would love it if he were more confident and didn't look so awkward – for his own sense of belonging, not for me.

- I wish he could hear difficult emotions without feeling threatened and without needing to withdraw – physically, verbally and emotionally – sometimes for several days.

- I wish he could understand the intricacies of situations and not need every tiny specific detail spelled out. I would like not to have to answer all his questions in his search for understanding of an endlessly complex social world and would like not to see him so confused and out of his depth.

- I wish he had a social life that he could come home and tell me about. I would like him to expand his world with new things and ideas from other people.

- I wish he felt sure enough to declare categorically that I'm the one for him and that he wants to spend his life with me without having to say that he's not sure and how could he possibly be expected to know something like that because he might change his mind or he hasn't met everyone in the world, and so on…

- I wish he wasn't so afraid of getting things wrong and would just go for it. His fear of failure paralyses him and prevents him from achieving his dreams.

- I wish he wasn't so scared of everything – me, life, people, making mistakes, being alone, being overwhelmed, being himself, being happy.

- I wish that things didn't have to be quite so on his terms most of the time, although I do know that he is doing the best that he can. He is committed but demonstrates this in his own way. It is not always easy for me to recognise or acknowledge it.

What works

Sarah: I try to keep things simple for Keith. I don't ask too many questions at once or make too many demands. It is a fact that many people with AS become overwhelmed easily and are literally unable to respond or react. A form of mental paralysis or shutdown seems to occur. I have known people take three or four minutes to reply to a question, sitting blankly for what seems like a very long time saying nothing. Eventually, an answer will come but they needed that length of time to process all of their thoughts. AS partners may need this level of patience applied to them too – it's not about either partner suffering to the detriment of the other.

Keith: True. Working out what to say can sometimes be horrendously difficult. It involves trying to determine all the combinations of how what you say can be interpreted when you know exactly what you mean.

Sarah: Arguing with Keith is totally pointless because he seems unable to communicate or hear difficult feelings without withdrawing. That's not to say that it doesn't happen! Shouting, crying and becoming very emotional confuses him and makes it impossible for him to respond in any way at all. I invariably feel worse, so it doesn't really benefit me either. Using scales of 1–10, as mentioned earlier, to gauge the level of importance he places on things and to express our feelings about things is much better for Keith. This really works for us. If I tell him I am a '9' stressed, he understands what that means better than a lot of crying and anxiety.

Anything perceived as criticism seems to be very damaging. I try to phrase things in a way that shows understanding of his views and input.

Keith: This is very effective for me. It is immediate and communicated to me in a language I can understand and without the shrieking. It is perfect for my needs. I don't find this simplistic or patronising. It simply works.

Sarah: If I have asked for some support and he has not provided it, aren't there only two possible options?

He won't do it because he doesn't want to.

He can't do it – for various reasons.

It may be that he doesn't know how to do it. With Keith I cannot assume that he finds something easy just because I do. Doing the shopping and planning a week's dinners causes huge anxiety from too many choices or the fear that he will get it wrong, or he may just forget because he has a naturally terrible short-term memory. I have to be confident that his not doing these types of things for me in no way reflects upon his feelings for me, so I have to learn not to take it personally (again!).

Keith: Others appear to sail through life with ease in a way that I cannot. Decisions and tasks that appear to be easily executed by others can reduce me to complete mental paralysis. This, combined with my poor memory, results in me forgetting and struggling to do all that I should. This is no measure of my feelings for Sarah and is not idleness on my part. The possibility of failure or getting it wrong is very difficult and stressful and prevents action.

Sarah: We have tried using problem-solving to weaken his existing immovable beliefs by presenting alternative solutions. Some people with AS find it hard to see more than one perspective. Keith and I wrote down all the possible options to his main goal (giving up work and going to live in France) and then wrote the pros and cons of each option. He found this a real eye-opener and he could see on paper what choices he had. This really worked for him.

Keith: This was very revealing. In my world there is usually one answer to any problem. If this answer does not allow me to do what I want, I will stop thinking about the issue altogether. Doing this exercise let me see that there were lots of possible solutions, each with their own pluses and minuses and I am able to consider each one. I would never have been able to contemplate this previously.

Thoughts for non-AS partners: Sarah

- Doing the Autism Quotient, Systemising Quotient and Empathy Quotient (Baron-Cohen 2003) was really interesting. This brought it home to me how differently we think and react to situations and how different our ideas are. How can I be angry at someone who so clearly sees things in a different way? Neither of us is wrong, just different. This made the whole thing very real for me to look at his answers in comparison to my own.

- I gave Keith a copy of *Men Are from Mars, Women Are from Venus* (Gray 1993). He was staggered to learn that women feel better just by talking and that sometimes all he was required to do was listen – not offer solutions and sensible advice. By giving him a book (evidence), I was able to convince him that it was not just me who felt this way, but many women. There is a lot in John Gray's book that explains differences between men and women generally, and as the autistic man is said to have an extreme male brain (Baron-Cohen 2003), then this advice will particularly suit him. I found it useful in looking at expectations and understanding his behaviour. The concept that men and women speak different language seems applicable here.

- Even though these things may not feel particularly important to me, Keith shows me that he cares by repairing my bike and carrying my shopping. It has been helpful for me to recognise that these are things that he knows he can do well, will not fail at and so feels confident in doing them. I try to tell him what would be helpful or useful in practical ways. This may feel more solid for him than abstract gestures like flowers or displays of affection. I try to find things that he is confident in doing and don't expect him to do things he is not sure of, as he expects to fail. None of us would want to do this. When I let him be successful he feels better about trying more things in the future.

- I spent a long time trying to become perfect in the hope that he would change and everything would be rosy. I made life hard for myself and continually failed. It is healthier for me to be myself and look after my own best interests. I am only responsible for 50 per cent of this relationship. If it doesn't work, it will not be entirely my fault.

- I realised that I am getting more of him than anyone else. He may well be giving all he can. Who can ask for more than that? No one person can meet all my needs. I have to find other sources for emotional support, socialising if he cannot do it.

- If he is happy, accepted and not anxious, he can be the best that he can be – and that benefits me. Putting excessive demands on him causes more withdrawal, anger and frustration, for both of us. Yes, it can feel unfair, but I ask myself if I would be able to do something that felt uncomfortable to me.

- I make sure I appreciate everything he does, tell him how happy I am and how great he is – even if I don't feel like it at that moment. This requires a concerted effort to begin with but becomes second nature. This has made such a massive difference to the way he sees himself. He says he doesn't believe me when I say these nice things to him, but his whole self has changed into a more confident, better-dressed, more sociable, reciprocating man – as opposed to the 'boy' I first met. I believe that to receive so much positive feedback must have an effect over time. Small effort from me leads to major shifts in him. This is what he has learned to do for me to similar great effect. Perhaps that is the key to a successful relationship – make an effort and notice and appreciate the good bits in each other.

- Both of us learning as much as possible about AS has been crucial. I ask him questions about how he sees things and get him to explain his thought processes to me. This encourages him to examine his own logic and become more self-aware. If the questions are asked in an enquiring way rather than a negative one, then he will happily tell me the goings-on of his mind all day long.

- Communicating clearly. Things often need to be worded in a specific way in order for him to understand. It is easy to think he is being deliberately stupid and obstructive, but this is not the case. If I am not getting my message across, this is my problem as the communicator, not his. This often gives me headaches trying to rephrase things time and time again.

- I tell him immediately if he has said or done something that I find inappropriate. This stops me saving things up for hurling at a later date, by which time he cannot remember what he said or did. He gets confused that I said nothing when he did something six times then on the seventh blew my top. This is too inconsistent for him. He says he cannot learn new ways of social behaviour unless he is told immediately. We do this by a light punch on the arm. It is immediate, not perceived as negative and doesn't involve lots of confusing words. Others may prefer a non-violent form of communication!

- I used to spend all of my energy on him trying to fix him, help him sort his life out. I used to send him books to read and website links to look at. He didn't ask for it and I would get annoyed that he didn't seem eternally grateful for my advice and often didn't use it. There are piles of unread books in his flat all sent by me. I would be infuriated if someone kept offering me unsolicited advice and sending me books to tell me how to improve myself. So, I stopped. I changed my focus on to myself and decided to fix myself instead. If he needs that many upgrades, I should look for a better model. I still suggest things of interest to him and then I drop it. Interestingly, since I have done this, he takes up a lot more things on his own. I guess he feels he has some power and choice rather than being bullied and cajoled. I have been a parent since the age of 19 and so in a caring role. I have to restrain myself from interfering. This is hard when he can be so willing to sit back and let me take over. This involves a conscious effort not just to do everything and then become resentful and moan about it.

- Being myself. Not walking on eggshells. This is harder than it sounds, but ultimately why be with someone who I cannot be myself with? I have done this for a long time out of fear that if I was myself and stood up for what I wanted, he would decide I was not suitable and leave. It hasn't happened. Since I have been more honestly assertive, rather than emotionally manipulative to try and get my needs met, I am happier and he is happier. He never asked me to tiptoe around him, but his insistence on his own rightness and my wrongness made me fearful, I think. We have fewer arguments now as I am not in need of constant reassurance – an unattractive trait. I have the confidence to know that I must be myself, even if it is at the risk of losing him.

- If there are things that I find easy, but that he struggles with, I do them. I don't mean big life-changing things that he needs to cope with himself, but small things. Why see him stressed when it's not necessary. I try to take the load off when I can. I know he does the same for me. It is about noticing what we can do for each other, not keeping tabs on who's done what, but trying to make life easier for us both.

- I don't ask loaded questions or make emotional statements expecting a response. Saying 'I love you' in the hope he will say it in return is doomed to failure and disappointment. He may not realise it's expected of him and may not feel like saying it at that precise moment, so he won't. He may have said it in 1982 and doesn't see the need to keep on repeating it. None of this means he doesn't love me. This is non-AS game playing and reassurance and he doesn't know the rules.

- If my mental or physical health were compromised in any way, I would leave. He may not be able to 'help it' and it may not be intentional, but the end result would be the same –

that I am harmed by being in a relationship with him. I may be the only person in his life and know that he will be totally isolated and depressed without someone being there. He may tell me that it is all my fault and that I am the one with the problem, but I would have to be confident that if it's not OK for me then it's not OK – regardless of what he says. I am not wrong because I don't agree with him and I am responsible for remaining.

- I have to admit that there is a pay-off for me in having a partner who doesn't go out much without me. I don't have to deal with my own insecurities about where he is or who he is meeting. He doesn't flirt (wouldn't know how), doesn't get drunk and doesn't go out anywhere at all really.

- I have to take full responsibility for being here. I choose to remain. It is wrong of me to complain about my lot, when I have created it. Remembering this allows me to stop feeling like the helpless victim and see that I have the power to decide what happens in my life, regardless of him or what he would prefer. Just because he doesn't like it, doesn't mean I won't do it – it's my choice.

- I remember why I fell for him. It's all still there. Perhaps life has overloaded him so much that he can no longer be that person anymore.

Thoughts for AS partners: Keith

- Know that you can offend merely by telling the truth. That's hard and it's a huge responsibility. This doesn't mean that you have to lie, but it does mean you should avoid concentrating on the singular question that has been posed. Try some context. Mostly, people ask questions that are specific, but which are actually not isolated and fit into a bigger picture. It's hard always to know what this picture is, especially if the question itself seems critical. So, if a question evokes some level of discomfort, try discussing the context of the question before answering. This doesn't capture all the potentially harmful questions that result in upset, but it's a start!

- Small things that demonstrate caring make a huge difference.

- Do whatever you can for your partner – and do it often!

- In spite of my self-righteousness, the majority of the time I'm wrong!

- It might be tiring for all concerned, but – ask. Ask if it's OK. Ask for more information. Ask what is required of you.

- Listen and be prepared to be astonished. Know that others think differently!

- The more uncomfortable I become, the more reliant I am on my preconceptions. For example, the more my viewpoint is challenged, the less able I am to be receptive to different opinions. I forget that I am the minority, the one with the difference, and hold my position more firmly. This is not always helpful.

CHAPTER 12

Conclusion

Impressions of others

Sarah: It's interesting to see how we look from the outside and whether we appear noticeably different or unusual. I asked a few people who have seen us together. Their comments are entirely unedited. Several factors make this a biased study. First, due to our only being able to spend weekends together, we tend to spend these alone together and I do most of my socialising outside of that time. Whether the situation would be any different were we to live together, I can't say. Second, I don't really know many people who have conventional relationships (if there is such a thing). I have a friend whose ex-husband is now living with her again (platonically) after five years apart. I have another friend who has a partner of four years and they do not live together. I know many people in their 30s and 40s who are not in long-term relationships, either divorced or never married, with or without children. Third, like me, many of my friends work in the voluntary sector with people with disabilities, neuro-diversity and differences of various kinds. Our level of professional tolerance is high, therefore, things which may be deemed strange by some rarely cause a raised eyebrow when you spend your days with people who display a wide range of atypical behaviours. Hence, Keith is accepted for who he is. I do remember his mum saying that he was very different when he was with me and that she was so pleased to see him happy.

Karen (close friend and Sarah's housemate of three years): You have the strongest relationship of our peer circle and laugh more than almost anyone I know – and that is very striking. Socially, I have noticed that

Keith does look awkward and it is clear that you keep things comfortable for him by making sure he is OK. I am in a similar relationship myself and am aware that it often appears to others that the non-AS partner is controlling the relationship, but this is due to the needs of the AS partner. They often need things to be controlled, taken care of so they don't have to take any more responsibility than necessary as they will become overloaded. In reality, in social situations, it is the AS partner who is calling the shots.

Frank (Sarah's brother): It's clear that some of the things he does irritate you, but I've never heard you scream at him like you used to with your ex-husband. Keith is likeable but doesn't give much away about himself.

Fiona (close friend of Sarah's for five years): As a couple you seem physically matched and always look happy, very attentive to each other, in your own little bubble. Does he appear different? Not overtly, he's quiet in large groups, but so are lots of people. Clicky fingers are weird, but I've always found him friendly. I know more from what you've said than what is apparent from seeing him or being in his company. Is it unequal? I think initially you nagged/henpecked to try and mould him, but it didn't work and he just walked. Since your work with Asperger's you've been more accepting, but it seems that Keith has changed and become more adaptable too. You each bring different things to the relationship: you are more sociable and eloquent, while Keith is better with facts/statistics, designing your website, answering email enquiries for you. It appears that you both pull together and each have areas where you help one another, but I wouldn't say there is an overriding boss. You would be the obvious boss, but he wouldn't have it!

Final words

Sarah: As with all relationships, communication is the key. It feels like translating another language at times, with the requirement that each party openly embraces the other's difference in understanding and interacting with the world. I believe it was Lorna Wing who said 'Throw out what you know and start again'. If we are willing to do this and deal with the discomfort it brings, we may stand a better chance at knowing what is going on in each other's minds.

The other aspect is simply to appreciate each other for who we are and what we do. This is not always easy when overloaded with work, life, children and other daily concerns, but it seems that a small amount of effort to make someone feel good can have a huge effect over time – it may take time to reverse some of the negative input that has been received in the past. We would both concur to this. How hard can it be just to be nice to the person you love?

Who knows what the future holds. There are no guarantees in life – with or without AS. Keith finds my occasional 'emotional fraughtness' and 'demands' difficult. I find his 'cold harshness' and 'my way or no way' approach difficult. We both find the prospect of losing someone unique and special even more difficult. I have no desire to change or 'fix' him; I wouldn't change anything about him (apart from stopping that awful bone-cracking!). There is no wrong or right, just people trying to navigate an acceptable middle way. I hope that we have been able to share something of some value. The last words go to Keith, without whom this book, or the person I am today, would not have been possible.

Keith: Communication is vital. I have learned to listen, to accept and to compromise. I have learned that my small efforts make a big impact. The big impact is that I retain what I want in a stress-free environment. The learning has been by both of us, though: Sarah has applied her understanding that I will respond to pressure completely opposite to the manner she had intended – she now communicates her feelings in such a way that doesn't sound critical, emphasises benefit and is easy for me to relate to. Making our relationship simple has allowed me the freedom to enjoy what we have.

I had to learn about Asperger syndrome. I had to acknowledge that it makes me different and difficult by social norms. I had to understand it limits my suitability as relationship material. Sarah learned all of this, too. Combined with an ability to recognise a good thing, this knowledge has meant we are able to retain our desire to be around each other.

Acceptance of Asperger syndrome has put my life into perspective. Previously I felt completely isolated and didn't know why and took the blame for it. Sometimes I could take it on the chin, mostly I couldn't. Now I know I'm not to blame, I have an explanation. My outlook on life now is that I have life.

References

American Psychiatric Association (APA) (1994) *Diagnostic and Statistical Manual of Mental Disorders,* 4th Edition. Washington, DC: American Psychiatric Association.

Aston, M. (2003) *Aspergers in Love.* London: Jessica Kingsley Publishers.

Aston, M. (2005) *Cassandra Affective Disorder.* Accessed on 20 March 2007 at www.maxineaston.co.uk/cassandra.

Attwood, T. (2002) *Why Does Chris Do That?* London: National Autistic Society.

Attwood, T. (2006) *The Complete Guide to Asperger's Syndrome.* London: Jessica Kingsley Publishers.

Baron-Cohen, S. (2003) *The Essential Difference: Men, Women and the Extreme Male Brain.* London: Penguin.

Garnett, M. and Attwood, T (1998) 'The Australian Scale for Asperger's Syndrome.' In T. Attwood (ed) *Asperger's Syndrome: A Guide for Parents and Professionals.* London: Jessica Kingsley Publishers.

Gillberg, C. (1991) 'Clinical and neurobiological aspects of Asperger syndrome in six family studies.' In U. Frith (ed) *Autism and Asperger Syndrome.* Cambridge: Cambridge University Press.

Grandin, T. (1995) *Thinking in Pictures.* London: Bloomsbury.

Gray, J. (1993) *Men Are from Mars, Women Are from Venus.* New York: HarperCollins.

Holliday Willey, L. (1999) *Pretending to Be Normal.* London: Jessica Kingsley Publishers.

Holliday Willey, L. (2006) 'To Tell or not To Tell, That is the Aspie Question.' In D. Murray (ed.) *Coming Out Asperger.* London: Jessica Kingsley Publishers.

Murray, D. and Lesser, M. (2006) 'Confidence, Self-confidence and Social Confidence.' In D. Murray (ed) *Coming Out Asperger.* London: Jessica Kingsley Publishers.

Sanderson, S. (1994) *Student Vegetarian Cookbook.* London: Foulsham.

Shattock, P., Savery, D. and Whiteley, P. (1997) *Autism as a Metabolic Disorder.* London: National Autistic Society.

Slater-Walker, G. and Slater-Walker, C. (2002) *An Asperger Marriage.* London: Jessica Kingsley Publishers.

World Health Organization (2005) *International Statistical Classification of Diseases and Health Related Problems,* 10th Revision, Second Edition. Geneva: Nonserial Publications.

Resources

Asperger Training
Our website. We give talks and presentations together on relationship issues. Sarah, as a professional trainer, also delivers training courses, seminars and presentations on a number of Asperger syndrome related topics. The site also contains information about AS.
www.asperger-training.com

ASPIRES
Online resource for family members and partners of individuals with autistic spectrum disorders. There are articles from various authors on different aspects of the condition.
www.aspires-relationships.com

House in Morocco
Keith's first attempt at designing a website for Sarah's holiday home for rent in Morocco.
www.houseinmorocco.com

Maxine Aston
Maxine counsels couples where one of the partners has, or both have, AS. She also runs workshops for women displaying the effects of sharing their life with such a partner. She has defined the condition 'Cassandra Affective Disorder' to classify these symptoms.
www.maxineaston.com

National Autistic Society
Huge website containing large amounts of information on all aspects of autism. There are specific sections on AS.
www.nas.org.uk

35317409R00081

Made in the USA
San Bernardino, CA
21 June 2016